# THE MEANING
# OF FINDING COINS

# THE MEANING OF FINDING COINS

## Messages and Spiritual Insights

KIMBERLY AHRI

AHRI

Publishing

Printed in the United States of America

ISBN-13: 978-0692972984
ISBN-10: 0692972986
Library of Congress Control Number: 2017916669
First Edition: November 2017

*Wonder is a
celebration for the soul.*

# Table of Contents

## Chapter 5:
## Financial Reassurance

## Chapter 6:
## Creating Space for the Wonder of Life

## Chapter 7:
## Coin Intervention: A Living Life Review

# ✧ Introduction: My Story

When I was young, my mom told me that pennies were from Heaven. In my twenties, when my dear grandfather passed away, Mom's penny finding took on a deeper, more personal meaning. Now when she found a coin she'd hold it up between her thumb and index finger and announce with a smile, "It's from Pop."

At the time my thoughts were, I'll admit, pretty condescending—along the lines of, "How nice for her that she believes such a thing." I thought it was just a made-up way to still feel connected to her father, like wishful thinking. I understood the desire, but it seemed to me that she was reaching.

Back then, when I saw pennies on the street, I'd walk right by them. Of course, I'd heard the saying "Find a penny, pick it up, all day long you'll have good luck," but I never had any noteworthy good luck streaks as a result of finding coins.

A penny in the street?

Big whoop.

Much bigger things were needed to catch my interest. Things like everything going my way, or me getting the new house, the new car, or the fat raise I wanted. Now *that* was the kind of luck I was looking for.

I rolled my eyes at my mom's more expansive spiritual view of life, encouraging her to not talk about "those sorts of things" in front of others, lest she be taken for a nut job. I did my best to discount any divine experience I had myself because the extraordinary was uncomfortable, even threatening. I wasn't ready.

Where I found comfort was inside my business brain. That part of me dominated. Starting as early as my teens, I had used my obsessive focus on working and material goals to distract myself from the callings of my soul.

It served me well to live "left-brained" — thinking, analyzing, using reasoning skills to foster the tough mental shell that protected me in what I perceived to be a cruel world.

So, how does a woman like that come to write a book like this?

Something happened to me.

I mean, SOMETHING HAPPENED TO ME.

At age thirty-seven, my views began to radically

shift when EVERYTHING about my life began to change. I had a breakthrough preceded by a total, life-as-you-know-it breakdown.

My detail-driven mind began to give way, yielding to another equally strong part of me: the creative/intuitive part. It was almost as if the right brain said to the left brain, "Look, you've had her for thirty-seven years. It's my turn. Step aside."

Now!

An angelic experience helped me change my course. Then, a serious health scare left me feeling like I was at death's door. And even though I was free of chemical influences, like alcohol or prescription drugs, my mind began to short circuit. I started experiencing cognitive difficulties. Activities that were once second nature became extremely difficult, brain-wrenching tasks.

This wasn't my first go-round with brain challenges. At other peak stress times in my life, from around age eighteen, again in my mid-twenties, then again at age thirty, there were periods when my brain ceased operating the way it normally did. Each time the episodes lasted a little longer and progressed in terms of the severity of my symptoms, but I was able to recover, probably because I had the resilience of youth on my side.

When the cognitive challenges appeared again at age thirty-seven, life as I had known it ceased abruptly. Can you imagine waking one day and realizing that you don't know your own brain anymore?

I could no longer handle details, numbers, or finances without my brain thrashing about. This was a huge problem considering that I'd spent the last twenty-plus years, that is, my entire career, in the mortgage industry specializing in...you guessed it: details, numbers, and finance. The brain that could once handle the complexity of preparing to file corporate taxes could now barely pay a bill online.

I could no longer track with instructions. My short-term memory failed me. My long-term memory was spotty. I forgot how to do things I'd done well for years. Listening to a person read out loud, or to a car blinker *click-clicking* while I waited for the light to turn—these things now drove me nuts.

Life in the form that I'd built it was being demolished. I watched helplessly as everything that mattered to me at the time, namely my magical, multi-tasking mind, job title, career, businesses, home, rentals, material possessions, financial security, the ability to produce income, and even my highlighted hair and fake, glossy fingernails—everything I tied my worth to—was being lost. And with it went my identity. Who would I be without these things?

I had no clue what my life would look like or how I'd take care of myself. There was much to grieve. Somewhere along the way, a gentle voice spoke to me in my head. It shone like a beacon of light through the darkness of fearful thoughts, informing me, "Sometimes those considered 'disabled' by society standards are actually ENABLED for their life's mission."

Right beyond all the tangible physical loss and the mental limitations I perceived, something was flourishing. The creative/intuitive part of me, the part previously bound and suffocated by my workaholic tendencies, had gleefully broken free of her restraints and run out from the shadows to stand in the spotlight of center stage. She claimed responsibility for all the words I could hear in my head.

There was talk of a book "in there" so I sat down willing to take dictation, to type the words I'd been listening to. I was used to being insanely busy — working twelve to fourteen hours a day busy. Comparatively, sitting on my behind and typing felt kind of like resting. So I tried to write, something I used to do as a kid for fun, something I hadn't done since.

When I began writing my worn-out spirit came alive again. I had found a purpose. As I immersed myself in this newfound source of joy, the migraines that I'd had daily for over ten years also yielded and became more infrequent. The truth is, those daily migraines were the self-absorbed filter that influenced my every perception. They had darkened my view on life and I wasn't used to feeling joy. They were also the measuring stick for whether I viewed myself as healthy or not. Without headaches, I thought, surely I must be healthy.

While their absence appeared to have left a thick residue that clogged my cognitive function, at the time, I expected that would resolve itself, just like it had in the past. So even though there was much to navigate within this new brain, I was grateful to have the writing outlet. I was pretty amazed by it since it was hard for me to grasp how I could write creatively when I often couldn't find words to speak out loud, chose the wrong words, or even accidently spoke blended words into made up combinations.

The brain was in charge. I wrote on creative brain days and put the manuscript away during the days or months when I was lucky to remember how to find my way home from the grocery store. This is how my first book was born. One of the most head-scratching things that still regularly happens when I'm writing is that words appear on the screen that I don't recognize. That's right. I see them and I don't even know what they mean. I look them up. They turn out to be correct. I shake my head with amazement. If it didn't happen to me I'm not sure I'd believe it was possible. That, ladies and gentlemen, is how amazing the brain is.

I implored my doctor to explain this to me. How am I able to write sometimes, when so much in there seems to be misfiring? "Different parts of the brain do different things," he told me.

It turns out when the "executive function" area is fussy and making it hard to navigate time or a simple daily activity, it's still possible for the creative part of the brain to sip from previous years of avid readership and spit forth accurate words onto a page.

I'll take it. On the days that I can write I "overjoice." I'm chuckling as I write that. I'm overjoyed and rejoice. Yeah. I'm going to leave that word there. One of my brain's made-up words has made an appearance. So the book you're holding is a miracle in my life, seven years in the making, one little pocket of "overjoicing" at a time. A labor of love.

As if all of that wasn't quite a lot, there's way more. Here's where things get really wild. Beyond being called to write, my brain was altered in a way that allowed for a new version of reality. The "extraordinary" I previously shied away from would become the norm.

First though, I entered a gestational phase. The energy of nuance and subtlety was the amniotic fluid I felt all around me. I would emerge from this phase overwhelmed by a new level of sensory perception, able to feel at a much deeper level and see what I wouldn't have noticed before. Like the neighbor boy in the movie American Beauty, I was now the type to be utterly taken in by the beauty of a plastic bag blowing in the wind.

Spiritual experiences had flickered around me all my life. I caught them out of the corner of my eye and intended to make them stay put—out there. I hadn't wanted to draw them closer and deal with what that might entail. Now I had a sense that I was MEANT to.

The most enriching part of my life's journey began. From the sheer desperation to understand my new brain, I went inward, beginning to work with and develop intuitive gifts that I'd had all along but had been frightened of.

There had been angelic encounters throughout my life. Once my willingness to listen was in place, almost immediately I began to receive profound and loving spiritual insight, as if the angels had been right there the whole time, ready to go, just waiting for me to allow their interaction. Over time, many avenues through which to see and listen would unfold.

One thing I'd like to say is that I've never considered myself to be "a channel." What I do is listen to inner wisdom; the source of which I believe is divine.

When I receive insight and guidance, I recognize the heavenly signature by its beautiful tone. The information always calls me higher. Without fail, it inspires and encourages behavior based in honor, compassion, peace, love, and forgiveness.

The prevailing themes involve serving the Creator through helping others, treating the self with tender care, listening to body wisdom, honoring the needs of the body, appreciating nature, finding joy, and embracing the wonder of life.

This Loving Source is continually emphasizing the ways in which we are all the same as humans, all benefiting from less judgment and more love. If there was one message I could boil it down to it would be:

***Be the love you wish to see in the world.***
***Act with, feel, and be love for yourself.***
***Act with, feel, and be love for others.***

(Love for yourself has intentionally been listed first. The idea is to care for yourself with honor and love so that those you help are being served by a WHOLE person exuding the energy of honor and love. Those who model good care of the self are needed in our society. This is a very different idea than what we've been taught: that it's "honorable" to deplete ourselves to serve others.)

In the beginning, after I'd gained some confidence with my ability to hear angels, a natural progression seemed to be offering angel readings. During a reading, I'd ask the angels questions on behalf of my clients about how they may better their lives.

Then came a time when I experienced what I've dubbed a "coin intervention," which encouraged me to re-evaluate my path. I gave up doing angel readings to focus on some health issues, felt relief, and noticed that I was no longer aligned with doing readings at all. So I didn't return to them. I just followed what felt right.

Ironically, when I made the decision to no longer request information, my gift of guidance expanded and grew stronger with each following year.

The distinction between information requested and information that arrives free of my request was significant to me at the time and still is. To the extent that I can, I want to free the whole guidance/insight phenomenon from my human will. My preference is to align with Source and allow space for wisdom, if it is so bestowed—not to keep asking for stuff. My intention is to serve God and love others.

During this phase I came to understand my life's mission: Using my own life and experiences as a backdrop, as honestly and authentically as I can, I'm supposed to share the insight and messages given to me. I was once told this was the reason for the vast number of experiences I've had—to gain compassion and understand more of the human experience so I may relate to others deeply.

I honor my mission by collaborating with the Divine. I pay attention when my tutors begin to teach. I'm excited, honored, and awed by what I am able to perceive. Then I try to find the best words I can to convey what I've been taught.

Throughout the book, you'll hear me use different words to describe the Source of the information I share—guides, angels, and the like. God has no shortage of loving messengers who wish to serve. As I mentioned, I've intended that it all originate with God's blessing. I view myself as a student of the Creator and the divinely designated tutors.

Those who know me personally will tell you that I do my best to live according to the information I'm taught, but I'm no different than you. I'm a work in progress; a real human just doing the best she can.

This book has been written because the coin intervention I experienced personally moved me to pay attention to the messages the coins have to offer. As it turns out, they offer a lot.

I will be sharing my personal experience, the stories and experiences of others, as well as the insightful messages and divine guidance I began to receive after publishing a post about coins on my blog many years ago. Once I directed my energy and thought toward the subject, a divine conversation began and has continued.

During the years since the blog post was published, I've been honored to be contacted by others compelled to share their story after reading mine. These stories are the kind that warm the heart and encourage the mind to open up to the wonder of life. I'm a huge proponent of the wonder of life as you will see.

On the blog I've also noticed a real hunger for explanation—is finding a dime or penny extraordinary in any way, or is it not? Is there really a phenomenon going on here? Or, is it just as simple and meaningless as someone else dropped their change?

I'm not claiming to be the Master Interpreter of Divinely Delivered Loose Change. However, if you're reading this book hoping that I'll shed some light on this mystery, if you are asking the question: Could there be a reason why I keep finding coins at the weirdest times or in the strangest places?—It is my intention to help you answer that.

If you're looking for science-backed literature, you can put the book down now. Smile. You won't find that here. While I have an interest in science, in our times there's just way too much muck to sort through in our search for personal truth. The message my guides encourage me to share is that the only thing you need to recognize truth is your own divine filter.

My spiritual experiences have taught me to honor your free will. Therefore, this book has been intentionally written to be open, rather than claim or define things as solid for you. I won't be the one who tells you, "If you see this, then this is what it means, period." Or, "This is what's going to happen, period." I write about potentials rather than definitives. My goal here is to empower you to feel your own answers, rather than try to influence you to see things as I do.

Thank you for buying this book and for coming on this spiritual journey with me. I pray it blesses your life the way it has blessed and added meaning to mine.

## Chapter 1

# The Invitation to a
## ✧ Divine Conversation

If I told you that picking up the random coins you come across could add a whole new layer of depth and meaning to your life, would you find that hard to believe?

I mean, *really*, is finding a quarter, or a dime, or a penny on the street a big deal?

Yeah. It really could be.

What if the coin, as you picked it up, gave you a sense of love and support that only your mom could give you, even though your mom's in Heaven now?

What if you suddenly felt able to let go of financial concerns that were plaguing you?

What if every time you found a coin in a most unusual way you understood that you'd just been invited to enter a state of wonder, enjoy the life-enhancing benefits of that wonder, and were able to relax into the soothing comfort of divine reassurance?

What if, from past experience, you knew that an oddly placed coin was sent as a loving reminder to take a step back and review what's going on in your life?

What if you knew the coin served as an affirmation that you're on the right track?

What if, over time, you came to believe that these remarkable experiences are actually part of ongoing communication from the divine realm? Would you feel less alone in this world?

**Would that add meaning to your life?**

It certainly has added meaning to mine.

This book is the result of one long chain of events. I experienced interesting encounters with random coins and I began to talk to others about what had been happening. When I brought up the subject to those who'd already had their own unique coin encounter, they smiled at me knowingly, eyes twinkling, eager to talk about it, like we were part of some special club.

Then, I wrote a post entitled *Is There a Spiritual Message in Finding Coins?* and put it on my blog. The post turned out to be some type of energetic call sent into the Universe to expand my awareness on the subject. (I later learned that I'd opened up what my guides call "an energetic pathway.")

I began to record the information that was being "downloaded" to me with the inkling it was meant to be a book.

The "download" was not just about coins. In addition to the meanings and possible reasons that people start to find coins in ways that are just plain hard to ignore, there was also an interesting blend of spiritual insight.

Some of the reasons people find coins you've probably already heard of. Some of the reasons will surprise you. Some of the spiritual insight may help you in daily life.

It's taken me years to get all this information together and while I originally thought the delay was only related to health issues, I now see that I needed to have quite a few years of experiences personally so my interpretation of what was occurring could expand.

Early on, I was mistaken about something important.

You see, at first I assumed that the only coins likely to contain a message were those found in truly remarkable ways, in the strangest of places, in the most apparent of patterns. I needed coins that were fabulously weird and bizarre and then as if on a treasure hunt, I'd try to figure out the hidden message.

On the other hand, if I found a penny next to a Coinstar machine, I didn't think much of it at all. A coin found there was to be expected. (If you don't know what a Coinstar is, it's a machine that people dump their bags of change into, the kind you might see in a grocery store. The machine sorts the change then spits out a ticket with a dollar count that they can turn in for cash.)

To this day, my favorite stories, like many within this book, involve the unusual and hard-to-explain because they contain the fun of mystical wonder.

What I've come to believe, however, is that those really strange incidents serve as the opening "invitation" to enter what evolves into a divine conversation. I think as you read through what follows, you may come to the same realization that I did...

Every coin does matter. Even the ones found in the most likely places, like by the cash register at the grocery store, or by the Coinstar machine. Yep, even those. Because if you wish to engage, they can become a part of a long-term conversation, one that will often reveal patterns.

So I shared this realization with others and invited them to see if their coin finding would expand. I watched with great interest as it did.

The simple act of picking up a coin can grow from *Eh, big deal* into a moment of wonder: *Wow, how in the world did that happen?* Which, after multiple moments becomes *Hey, I think there's something going on here*. Which, with your continued participation in picking up coins becomes the belief *There's definitely something going on*. Which then evolves into knowing that you're being watched over and offered support. Which turns into a sense of comfort that you can experience **every single time you find a coin.**

Interested?

You've probably already been invited to this conversation.

## What Does "An Invitation" Look Like?

Here are some examples of instances in which you may be receiving communication:

o   You find a coin where you're positive there was none before.

o   Multiple times, you find coins in odd places.

o   You have trouble explaining to yourself how the coin arrived. The circumstances are that unusual.

o   A coin arrived "out of thin air."

o   You find coins every day for a condensed

19

period of time.

o You find a coin after thinking about a loved one. It feels as if the coin is in reply to your thoughts.

o You think about how long it's been since you found a coin and then find one right away.

o You find the same denomination over and over. Just dimes. Just quarters. Just pennies.

o You asked a dying loved one to give you a sign that they're still with you. Once they pass over you begin finding coins in all sorts of random places.

o You recently lost a loved one and as soon as they passed, you couldn't help but notice coins everywhere.

o You often find change on the ground when you are concerned about your finances.

o You have a hectic lifestyle, or are overwhelmed, yet it's entered your busy awareness that you're seeing coins everywhere.

In the chapters that follow, we're going to explore some of these unique circumstances and their possible meanings. As mentioned, this book also includes the related spiritual insight offered to me in complement to the coin information. Here comes one now...

## Spiritual Insight: Your Divine Filter

My guides have explained to me that our world is in transition. The old ways are not producing peace and satisfaction. Many people are awakening and realizing that what we've been told is truth or what has been "proven" is not necessarily truth.

There is a better way.

We are moving toward becoming a society that places value on our instinct and our "knowing" over "proving."

When we were born, we all came standard with our own built in B.S. detector—gut instinct. But as we grow up, we learn to place more value on the offerings of our thinking mind. We're encouraged to identify with our minds and learn to believe what we've been told to think.

The trouble with using the "thinking mind" to discern what's true for us is that it's susceptible to being swayed by many types of input. The thinking mind can be affected by debate, popular opinion, and by our need to conform and fit in so we feel safe. It's also affected by artfully crafted sales campaigns, the intentional spin of political rhetoric, by scientific studies later proven to have been manipulated (with tobacco and GMOs, for example), by false news reports, by family influence, and the like.

As we transition to a "knowing" society, we free ourselves. There is no swaying or debating the gut. Individuals will learn to FEEL what is true for them by running all input through their own divine filter.

The best way to strengthen your filter is to use it. Rather than take opinions from others, simply ask yourself: Does this add value to my life? Does this feel right?

This book will be great practice!

## *Spiritual Insight: Determining What's True for You*

I'm going to offer you plenty of information for that amazing and wise filter of yours. There's no intuitive, psychic, scientist, or card reader whose opinion is superior to your own personal instinct.

YOU are the expert on the meaning of your own signs. Please do not allow me, or anyone else, to define what your moments of awe should mean to you. The only things I can offer you in this book are general in nature. And you, well—you are quite unique.

As you read through the text, I encourage you to consider the different messages and try them on.

Does one feel right to you? Does the story you're reading give you warm ripples through your body because you feel the same way or the same thing happened to you? Do the words feel expansive and welcoming? Does this new idea or potential belief enhance your life? Does it make you feel more alive? More excited about life?

Or, are you anxious and nervous and feel like you're trying to sell yourself on what you've just read?

To use your divine filter for your highest benefit, simply allow in what feels right to you, what resonates with you, and let go of the rest.

You can trust yourself to discern.

You can feel truth at a gut level.

What appeals to you is for you.

What feels right for you is right for you.

Now, let's get this party started with one of the most common reasons that folks find coins—their loved ones want to stay in touch.

## Chapter 2

# ✧ Coins Sent by Loved Ones

The Message

If you begin to find coins in very interesting ways after the passing of a loved one, consider this message:

> *While you may not see me in the physical, my spirit is alive. Our connection is eternal.*
>
> *A coin placed on your path carries not only my love, but also my hope that you will experience awe-filled moments and enjoy life. Know that I love you and I am with you.*

Love not only continues once we reach the other side, it also expands. The soul returns to its original, more divine perspective and is re-endowed with the full comprehension of what it means to be loved unconditionally.

While souls do retain personality traits, they will also merge with this love vibration, which is a true homecoming. For those they left on this planet, not only can they now see and feel the complexity of the real you, they also have the benefit of knowing what it's like to be human. Therefore, what you go through during your remaining human experience, is seen, felt, and understood with newfound depths of compassion.

Within this realm of love and wisdom, the soul is now able to consider the way they affected and interacted with others while they were here on Earth. Coins provide a way to continue interacting, an inlet through which to offer their love and support. The support through coins can be extremely impactful, as we will see in the stories that follow. They can provide nourishment for the spirit and offer a boost just when it's needed most.

## Alice's Story:
## Dimes from Heaven

If there's a story that captures the sentiment of "love from above" it's the story of Alice Lee, widow of David Lee. She wrote me in June of 2014 to share her story. Alice's powerful, heartbreaking story is also a beautiful testimony to love that endures from this world to the next.

I'm honored to share it here. Thank you, Alice.

"On Thanksgiving morning in 2009, my husband, David, died tragically on our honeymoon in Maui. He drowned in the

26

ocean while he was snorkeling. I never imagined that "till death do us part" would come just twelve days after we were married. I was devastated. I waited all my life to be married for the first time, only to become a widow less than two weeks later.

Shortly after my husband's death, I started randomly finding dimes everywhere I went. At first when I found the dimes, I would just put them into my wallet, not thinking it meant something special. After about the fourth dime, I thought it was strange that I kept coming across dimes within such a short period of time. Now it didn't seem so random to me after all, so I decided to save them and keep track of each finding.

After a while, I began to make some meaningful and symbolic connections with the findings. Each dime brings me a little moment of joy and some even give me goosebumps. At times when I am feeling particularly down and lonely, I find a dime along my path.

On many occasions, I would feel compelled to look in a certain direction and end up seeing a dime on the ground.

I've found dimes while traveling to other states and countries on vacation. I've found dimes at the store where I buy flowers for my husband, right before visiting the cemetery. These are just a few examples. As of today, I have found 464 dimes.

I believe these "dimes from Heaven" are signs from my husband to comfort me and let me know that he's still with me. The dimes have helped in the healing of my broken soul.

Also, now that my husband is not around in the physical, I have some uncertainties with the everyday decisions that I make. Whenever I find a dime in these situations, I feel reassured that I have David's support and it helps to validate that I'm on the right path.

This dime-finding journey has taught me to have a little faith (something I felt I'd lost when my husband died) and to believe that anything is possible. It has reminded me that even when you believe all is lost in your life, there is still hope if you keep your eyes and heart open to the signs around you."

The coin-finding experiences like what Alice describes are energetic in nature, which means they are full of layers and nuances. The dime serves as a key encoded with an energetic message. You unlock the message as you pick up the coin meant for you. The experience is no longer as flat as a dime. It can now open up to the energetic equivalent of 3D in surround sound. This allows for a full divine experience abundant in many insights, feelings of comfort, and "sudden knowing," as Alice's story illustrates.

## Gail's Story: In Memory of Rita Miranda Posey

This lovely story was submitted by Gail Posey Allen. I am inspired by the family's decision to take their mother's tradition and turn it into her legacy.

"Since my mother, Rita's, passing, dimes seem to always show up when we need her guidance, need extra prayers, or face challenges that we would have turned to her for help with.

We were (are) a very large family. There were ten of us children, so you can imagine that our mother had to stretch every dime.

Throughout my mom's life she collected dimes. She laughed when she found dimes in the wash and saved every one. With love and a smile, she was also known to charge us each a dime for a favor.

When times got tough, Momma never showed it. She was always generous, turning to her dime stash if she saw someone truly in need of help.

After she passed, I was amazed to see that over the years she had collected over $8,000 in dimes. Dad said whenever she reached a hundred dollars' worth he'd take them to the bank for a hundred dollar bill.

Before she died, she asked me to be in charge of her dime money and make sure that it went to a good cause. So I donated the money to the Gabriel Project, which is a Catholic Care Project for unwed mothers.

Since her passing the family has continued to collect dimes throughout the year and on the anniversary of her death, we donate the dimes to the Gabriel Project."

When I contacted Gail to see if she'd like her story included in the book, she followed up with:

"The Lord truly does work in strange and wonderful ways. It was only yesterday that I was retelling the story of why our family collects dimes to my grandchildren. It's coming up on Momma's "Heaven birthday" and I was rolling the dimes when they came over, as I will be giving them to the Gabriel Project next week!

Our family continues to grow. We're around seventy grandchildren and great grandchildren. Momma sends dimes their way now as well.

I love sharing Momma's story and would love to honor her in any way possible. I would also love to encourage others to know they can make a big impact with what may seem like so small a gift/donation."

## Cindy's Story: Dimes from Danny

Cindy Brooks Ficcaro's story is another example of continued communication with a loved one after passing. In this case, Cindy's boyfriend Danny, who's now on the other side, is able to carry on a sweet tradition he began during their earthly relationship.

"I used to tell my boyfriend, Danny, that finding dimes was a spiritual thing.

When he was alive, if he went out of town he would hide them for me to find while he was gone.

Since Danny passed away, I have found

dimes in the weirdest places—in the sand, behind displays, on a table that I was going to sit down at to listen to a band.

When I found a Canadian one (he was Canadian) in the parking lot near my Jeep, I started saving them.

I've noticed that when I have problems with my Jeep I find dimes from Danny. A couple of months ago I had Jeep problems twice and found two dimes. Today when I had to get a new battery, I found a dime.

Last weekend, I went to the Syracuse Winterfest with friends and we rode the city bus. I found a penny when I was getting off. While I was telling my girlfriend it didn't count since it was not a dime; right then her friend bent down and found a dime.

It should have been mine. LOL."

To my way of thinking, the dime her friend found could be considered a direct response to Cindy's statement that pennies don't count. I could almost hear him saying, "All right, how about this then?" Go Danny!

## Denise's Story:
## I Hear You and I'm with You

This heartwarming story was shared with me by Denise Lobsitz Gross. It offers us the comfort that our loved ones still hear us and know what's going on in our lives after they have passed on.

"After my father passed away, I was upset that I hadn't spoken with him about sending a sign of some sort once he was on the other side. I had thought of asking for a certain song that I'd be able to hear on the radio, or a coin. But, we didn't talk about it and time ran out.

I decided after he passed that every time I saw a penny it would be my way of stopping to think about him and send my love. However, it could only be a heads-up penny.

I soon started finding, or noticing, heads-up pennies. I'd pick them up, hold them and smile, then put them in my pocket for my collection.

When I was moving from my second-story apartment last year, I went up and down the stairs numerous times loading my car. I recall thinking, *I wish my dad were here because he would have wanted to hear all about my move and where I was going,* etc.

Twenty to thirty minutes after I wished my Dad was here to talk to, as I was making yet another trip up the stairs, I looked down and there on the step was a shiny, heads-up penny. The penny was not there before. I'd been up and down those stairs looking at each step for two hours. No one else was with me and the one other tenant who shared the stairway wasn't home.

I looked up to the sky beaming with love and excitement and said, "I know that was you, Dad."

It brings me solace to feel he heard me."

In Denise's case, not only did her Dad hear her, but he was also able to show her that he was present for her big move because she'd already set the intention to have pennies serve as proof of their continued connection.

## *Shari's Story: Coins for Jordan's Daughter*

This touching story was submitted by Shari Gose, Jordan's mother. It's about a father who has found a way to stay connected to his little girl using coins.

34

"My youngest son, Jordan, would drop money on the floor for his young daughter to find. It was a game played between father and daughter.

When he died in a car accident last summer I told his three-year-old daughter that when she finds money on the ground it will be money sent to her from her dad in Heaven.

It didn't seem that she was finding much so I would help out by leaving her some and she would exclaim, "Oh, money from Daddy... he wants me to be rich!"

One night she came for a sleep over. I vacuumed before she arrived. That night I went to bed late and was up before her in the morning. As I came out of my room I noticed a coin in her doorway.

I did some things around the house and when I went back to get her up I noticed more coins in the doorway and hallway. When she got up and started gathering coins, we found there was a trail of coins from her bedroom to the dining room, right to where her overnight bag was.

They weren't there when I got up and there was no one else home to leave them out. I know they are from my son to his daughter to let her know he is thinking about her."

Have you been finding coins and think they are from a passed on loved one? If you need some help figuring out who they might be from, we're going to talk about that next.

Chapter 3

# ✧ Who is Sending Me Coins?

If the answer to the question "Who sent this coin?" is important to you, try pausing at the time of occurrence and allow the answer to come. Your clues lie in the circumstance and how you feel. The steps below should help you.

Take note of the details. Let's say your dear departed father was obsessed with baseball. Dad's energetic signature might look like this: You were just talking about baseball when you spotted a shiny penny half hidden beneath leaves on a busy street. Or, you were not talking about baseball, but you stopped to pick a penny up in front of a baseball store. Or, you may have picked it up in front of a department store window displaying a jersey with Dad's favorite number or team on it.

Perhaps you didn't notice anything unusual at the time, but thinking back you wonder to yourself "Who sent this?" and then look up to see your Dad's smiling face staring back at you from a picture frame in your office. Trust yourself to know.

Your grandmother may say hello with a coin found beside her favorite flower, a random penny next to her picture on your bookshelf or a penny that falls out of a quilting book, if quilting was her thing.

Clues from circumstances are endless, but this is not about collecting irrefutable evidence. Your answer should come from an easy glance around. If your answer is there you'll know it when you see it. No straining of the brain required.

Does the date on the coin have any special meaning? Is it around the birth date or "eternal birth date" of a loved one?

Is the denomination symbolic of anything? If your mother collected dimes and you find dimes all the time now that she's passed, it seems pretty clear that Mom's sending them your way.

Quarters here in the U.S. stand to offer many clues. Over the years the design on the back has been changed to offer artwork and phrases related to each state.

If you find a Georgia peach coin and your loved ones favorite food was peaches, or one of their regular expressions involved calling others "a peach," that would be pretty clear, too.

In the state of California, the quarters released January 31, 2005 as part of the State Quarters Program have the image of John Muir on them with Half Dome as the backdrop and the words

"Yosemite Valley."

If I were to find this coin it would, without a doubt, bring with it the feeling of my dear friend Dick Derreberry, who crossed over years ago. While alive, his yearly trips to Yosemite—purposely made alone in January to camp in the snow—not only made me tease him about his sanity, but it also implanted within me a memory tying him to Yosemite.

One reader, a lady named Laurie, shared with me that while on vacation she went to do an activity that she and her mother liked to do together when her mother was alive.

During the activity that day, Laurie found a quarter at her feet. It was a commemorative quarter featuring the name of the town where her mother had grown up and also been laid to rest.

Now that's a big deal. Not to mention that Laurie had never even seen that type of quarter before.

The comfort from finding that quarter proved to be so significant it changed how Laurie felt moving forward in her life.

The answer to "Who sent me this coin?" can also be found in your feelings. Pause for a second when you find a coin and run a quick "feel check" through your body. As an example: My Nan washes a feeling of pure love and acceptance over me, a feeling I recognize from when she was alive and we were hanging out. (The smell of warm homemade bread also whisks me right back to the kitchen at my Nan's house. Smells are part of divine communication, too.)

You may also sense the personality of a passed loved one. An example: You find a dime in the strangest place and feel totally amused, just like you felt when your best friend was alive; she always knew what would amuse the heck out of you. I'd go with that feeling.

If cousin Vinnie, who is now passed on, was a total prankster in life and you just felt pranked when a couple pennies dropped out of thin air, then Vinnie's your answer. Oh, that Vinnie!

Take stock of what you've picked up.

A Penny?

Dime?

Nickel?

Quarter?

Make a mental note. It's not uncommon for patterns around specific denominations to develop. If you've got an Uncle Pat who has passed on and each year around the time of his birthday you begin finding nickels, that's Uncle Pat saying hello. Or you may notice that you find nickels whenever you reflect on his life, or come across pictures of him. If this pattern were to develop, I'd say you're experiencing ongoing communication. He wants you to know, "I'm still around you and offering my support to you."

With practice, it becomes easier to feel who is communicating with you. It gets so easy you may feel confident bypassing any "clues" and going straight to the easiest method of knowing. Simply ask the question in your mind, "Who sent me this nickel?" and then believe the first answer that comes to you.

If you do things the easy way, will the ego—the voice in your mind that promotes fear, negative views over positive thinking, and generally attempts to keep you focused on what's wrong instead of seeing the wonder of life—will that voice show up to talk smack? You bet. When you ask the question and the answer "Pat" quickly comes to you with no pomp and circumstance, the ego will tell you, "You're making it up."

I'm here to tell you there's a dazzling side of life waiting for you beyond ego input. It will continue to be there. And the ego will continue its attempts to cast doubt and skepticism. It's okay. If you're open to a life of sparkling wonder, your Creator will be with you as you move toward it. Moments of awe will be sprinkled on the earthen landscape around you. Each feeling of awe will build upon another until the day comes when even though you're still on Earth, your view of the world is totally different. A pattern to the happenings within the Universe emerges—what once appeared random is now seen in perfect order.

## Spiritual Insight: Opening the Energetic Pathway

Let's stay with the story of Uncle Pat and the nickels and go back to the ego that says, "You're not hearing from Uncle Pat. That's just wishful thinking."

What would happen if you decided that it's harmless to believe that dear Uncle Pat is checking in with you?

Not only is it highly likely that the incidents of finding nickels will increase, but your belief will also cause the limited views offered by your ego to begin losing power. Why? This is how energy stuff works.

You choose to believe and so you create. When you align with something, when you think it is so and believe it to be true, when you have genuine interest, that alignment opens up an energetic pathway.

This pathway not only emits an energy signal that works as an antenna to broadcast your interests into the ethers, but it also collects information, experiences, and events matching that signal frequency and using the same pathway, returns those energy matches to you.

More of the same energy begins to show up in life. At some point you've noticed this, right? For example, you decide to buy a new car and all of a sudden, you see the car you're considering purchasing everywhere.

Many humans call this type of thing coincidence, a term often used to brush off the occurrence as "meaningless." I consider the process to be much more divine in nature— *synchronicity*.

To take this concept a step further, the way you enlarge the energetic pathway—to bring more of what you're interested in to you—is by "investing" in it. You invest by taking action in the energy of it.

For example: A person considering a change in career would invest by researching the new career of their choice, maybe attending seminars on the subject, reading about it online, taking a local class, talking to others who do that work, listening to radio shows on the subject, and the like. With each action and energetic investment, we expand the pathway. Our signal to the Universe pulses stronger and more matching energy is returned to us.

**"Want" isn't an investment.** Action and spending time in the energy of what you desire is.

To keep a conversation with coins going, picking up the coins is the investment. Keeping a separate jar so you can see the coins grow in numbers and sharing your coin stories with others are also energy investments. As is reading this text.

## *Cathy's Story: Who Is Sending Me These Quarters?*

I'm excited to share this story that comes from Cathy DeMartino. She originally contacted me in May of 2012 to share her unique experience with finding quarters.

"Back in October 2011, my 88-year-old boss, who was like a Grandpa to me, passed away unexpectedly. He was a very wealthy man who had taught me much about business, money, investments, etc.

After he passed, I began finding quarters everywhere—all over my house, my car, my work, public places. So much so, I thought I was dropping the ones I found. My sister asked me what year was on them and I told her that I wasn't paying attention. This

44

prompted me to start looking at the year. The ones I found were all the same! 1967.

The year had no significant meaning to me and I couldn't think of how it may have been significant to my boss either. It wasn't a birth year or year of a family member's or friend's death. I wasn't even born until 1972. I just couldn't figure it out.

On my 40th birthday, my friends took me out to a club to celebrate. As we were standing in line to get in, I looked down on the floor. In front of the people in line ahead of us, there was a quarter. I jokingly said to my best friend, "Hey, pick up that quarter and tell me if it says 1967."

IT DID!!!

My friends looked very puzzled and asked...how did you know that? When I told them the story, we laughed. It made us all so happy. I really don't know what the significance of the year is, but I am always thinking of it. Either way, it brightens my day to know that someone up above is saying hello."

In December 2014, I was delighted to hear from Cathy again when she wrote to share this amazing follow up to her original story.

"Thanksgiving week, my family and I were camping at a local campground and while doing laundry in the camp laundry area (at midnight, in a storm because our camper leaked), my sister went to hand three quarters to my friend's son, Jonathan, to use for the dryer. One of them dropped in the grass. Because it was raining, cold, and dark out, he couldn't find it, so she handed him another quarter. I was watching this from a golf cart but I couldn't resist; I had to find that quarter! I never got up from the golf cart but I turned the flashlight on to look for it and saw it right away. It was near Jonathan's foot. I pointed to it with the light and asked him to pick it up and tell me what year it was. Of course, it was a 1967 quarter.

My sister knows the story, so we looked at each other, chuckled and smiled. I then explained the story to Jonathan. I told them both that I wish I knew for sure it was my former boss leaving them because I still can't figure out the significance of that year.

The next day, my husband and I ran into an old friend, Ken, at the campground office. Ken told me he had a present for me. When he was cleaning out his in-laws' house after they passed away, he found an old calendar from Cox Lumber Co., which is the company my late boss owned. Ken said he wanted to give it to me because he had saved it thinking it may be an antique. When I asked him what year it was, he said he thought it was 1967. My husband and I looked at each other and my eyes welled up with tears. So then I shared the story with Ken.

The next day, Ken had his daughter bring the calendar to camp. Sure enough, it was a 1967 Calendar! It meant so much to me. More than anyone will ever know.

I knew my old boss was confirming that it was him leaving me the quarters."

As many times as I have read Cathy's story, even knowing how it's going to end, it never fails to leave a smile on my face. Doesn't it also make you want to check the date on the coins you find?

What really stood out to me was that Cathy's dear boss wanted her to know, without a shadow of a doubt, that he's still around. Which bring us to our next topic: You are not alone.

Chapter 4

# ✧ You Are Not Alone

The Message

If you find coins during a time when you've been feeling alone in this world, please consider these messages:

> *Your Creator wants you to know, "I am watching over you and hear you."*
>
> *Your loved ones want you to know they are with you.*
>
> *Your angels and guides are with you and will guide you if you invite them to. Ask God to help you understand their guidance.*

As you read through the many stories in the book, there are some clear stand-out messages. The foundation that all messages rest upon is this: You are not alone.

In all that I do—in all that you do—we each have our own powerful support posse.

Should you engage with discerning the meaning of your found coins, you'll discover that you have loved ones, angel guides, spirit guides and a loving Creator waiting to communicate with you—to guide, provide comfort and support, to encourage and amuse you, as well as incite laughter, goosebumps, and feelings of awe. In short: to offer you that feeling of connection with "something more" that we all seem hard-wired to long for.

You live in a free-will Universe, blessed by choice. You give permission for these types of experiences to occur through the choices you make. What do you point your attention toward? What do you open your heart up to? Those are forms of permission.

Communication will always be offered. What expands a one-time, mind-boggling coin-finding experience into "ongoing conversation" is your genuine interest in fostering it.

## Spiritual Insight: Agreeing to the Coin Conversation

You don't need to "work" at it. It isn't hard to do. It's not something you need to pray about for days on end.

It's an agreement you make with the Divine Source that goes a little something like this:

*Yes, loving Creator of mine. I am interested and willing to allow myself to participate. I am willing to pick up the coins I find. I'm willing to notice a pattern, without pushing for one. I'm willing to be opened up further to the wonder and joy of life by feeling awe. I'm willing to look at finding change as if it's a special thing and willing to FEEL what the meaning is.*

## Dawn's Story: Continuing Reassurance

This story was offered to me by Dawn Niedetzki, a woman who has embraced the messages in the dimes she finds as continuing reassurance that she's being watched over and is never alone.

"I began to find dimes after my father died. It happened quite often and I found so many, I started keeping them in a canister. As grief subsided I found them less often.

Before my dad's passing, I had NEVER experienced anything like this. I knew nothing of this sort of thing. After finding so many coins and noting the significance, I started to look into the subject. When I told my son, sister, niece, and nephew about it, they also started to find dimes, although not as often as me.

We had another loss in the family five years after my father died. My sixteen-year-old niece unexpectedly passed away on St. Patrick's Day. Just as with my dad, the coins came the most often in the beginning and slowly tapered off once some healing had occurred.

I'm not sure how long after her passing this happened, but one St. Patrick's Day I went to the grocery store to get some Irish soda bread for the dinner I'd be making for my family that evening. Upon entering the store, the song *If I Die Young* by The Band Perry was playing, which reminds me of my niece. As I was looking around the bakery section, I heard a coin fall behind me and I thought to myself, "That's a dime! I know that's my dime!" I walked to where I had heard it and sure enough, there was a dime!

One time after the finding of the dimes had slowed way down, I began praying and talking to God while walking, asking why I hadn't found any for a while. As I was praying, right in the middle of the sidewalk was a shiny dime.

A week later, there was another dime leaning on the lint tray when I opened the dryer, then another one the next day, then a few days later one right next to my car.

There have been patterns and synchronicities. I often find them when I'm worried and take the coins to be messages of reassurance from my pops that I'm doing ok and that I'm headed in the right direction.

Finding a lot of dimes has a way of making a person go out looking for them. But it's when I'm not looking, when I'm thinking of a loved one or questioning my life and decisions (which is sometimes often for me) that I find them.

I find them when I need them the most."

Dawn's story is a great example of a person who noted the significance of the coins she was finding and whose genuine interest encouraged the conversation to expand. When I heard from her the first time she'd already found 51 dimes after her father passed and then another 54 following the passing of her niece.

She's also very blessed to receive reassurance from both her loved ones and from God. How wondrous to talk to God, and in what appears to be an immediate affirmation of His presence, find a dime.

## Cheryl's Story:
### Shiny Pennies from Bob

Thank you to Cheryl Eichner, who submitted this story. Her dear, departed friend Bob has been remarkably tenacious about reassuring her that he's still around.

"In January, I lost a lifelong friend named Bob. He was my husband's best friend and my best friend's husband. We were all high school sweethearts and grew up together.

Bob's death was sudden and a total shock. I felt that I needed to be strong for my husband and my best friend, so I ignored my own grieving.

Around the beginning of April when things with my husband and my friend started to settle down, I kept thinking about Bob.

One Saturday I couldn't get him out of my mind and I knew it was time for me to grieve. I went through a period of a few days, maybe a few weeks, when I'd cry and think of him.

It was during this time that I started finding pennies all around my house. I would leave one room and return to a bright, shiny penny lying on the floor.

At first I didn't think much of it. Maybe someone had a hole in their pocket or something, but it was always bright shiny pennies. I then remembered having watched TV's Long Island Medium, Theresa Caputo, tell a woman that when she found pennies it meant her loved one was leaving them for her. I told my mom about finding the pennies and attributed it to Bob but still I wasn't really convinced they were "Heaven sent."

A few weeks later, I stopped finding the pennies and mentioned this to my mom on a Sunday night. The very next morning I got up for work with only a nightgown on (without pockets) and while in the bathroom I heard something heavy fall to the floor and circle around and around. I kept looking and couldn't see what it was.

I checked to see if maybe a washer had fallen off the toilet or something was broken with the toilet. When I moved from looking, there was a bright, shiny penny lying on the floor where my foot was.

I was stunned and shocked and knew this was not a coincidence. We do not keep anything on the back of the toilet. There was nothing there when I came in. There is no explanation for where that penny came from.

I have decided to keep that penny as my lucky penny. I still continue to find bright shiny pennies around my house. They even show up in my robe pocket!"

I appreciate the multiple times and interesting ways that Cheryl's friend Bob made a connection using pennies.

A much simpler demonstration of connection is just as meaningful, especially when in direct response to how we are feeling on a certain day, like in this short and sweet story:

"Today was a lonely day and I was missing my husband who crossed over a few years ago. I went to put on my shoes and was surprised to find a dime inside one. Later in the day, I actually found another dime in a different pair of shoes! I decided to research whether there might be some meaning to this... "

If there was a day when I was feeling all alone and missing my loved ones, these coin-shaped tokens of love would touch my heart and mean the world to me.

## Mom's Story:
## A Dime in the Woods

This is my Mom's dime story.

"Years ago when my dad passed away, I started to find pennies, felt the connection to my father and decided to view them as pennies from Heaven, like my dad was saying hello.

When my Mom passed away years later, I began to find dimes and joked that Mom was trying to outdo Dad.

I have found many pennies and many dimes that touched me and carried the energy of my loved ones, but the time that stands out the most occurred after I made the trip home to visit family in Newfoundland, Canada.

My brother, John, and I decided to go for a walk in the woods with his five-year-old grandson, my great-nephew Max.

As we went deeper into the woods, out in the middle of nowhere, we came upon a picnic table. I'm not sure we would have gone near the table if Max hadn't headed over to it.

Right in the center of the table was a dime sitting there, waiting to be found.

I could feel the energy of Mom with us. It brought tears to my eyes as I remembered a conversation I'd had with her while she was alive. She'd been emphatic about how important it would be for me to continue making trips back to see my siblings once she was gone. Yet the trip is always a careful consideration, because it's a long one, all the way from California to Newfoundland and many times it isn't easy.

When we found the coin that day it was like she was letting me know that she knew we were there together, as a family, and that she was with us too!"

Mom's story is a perfect example of the message at the beginning of this chapter, "Your loved ones want you to know they are with you."

## Christina's Story: Pennies from Heaven

This goosebump-giving story was shared by Christina Mason.

"I was walking back to my house one day when I found a penny. I looked at the year, as I often do, and it was 1997.

This was of no significance to me so I thought to myself that it would have been better if it was one from 1998, since that was the year I lost my first son.

Next thing you know, I find my second penny. To my surprise, the year was 1998! I was totally amazed.

Still on my journey heading home, I then thought to myself how cool it would be to find a penny with either one of my daughters' birth year on it. (I have two daughters.)

Instantly, while thinking this, I found another penny. I was excited and nervous at the same time wondering what year this one would be...

It was a penny marked with the year my youngest was born!

At this point, I could not believe what was happening. I felt like I was dreaming.

I kept walking and was almost home. Of course, I now really wanted to find the last penny with my oldest daughter's birth year on it so when I got directly in front of my house I was a bit disappointed that I hadn't found it.

I wondered to myself if I should walk a bit more in the hopes of finding another penny with her year on it. Or should I just call it a day?

I decided to just give up and head up my driveway, thinking, "You can't have everything." In that very moment, I felt compelled to look to my left and of course, you can guess what I saw—a very shiny penny!

I kept staring at it saying NO WAY. Finally, I picked it up to see what year it said on it, and I could not believe my eyes—it was the year 2000. The year my oldest was born.

I was kind of freaking out now, but in a good way.

My kids' dad, Cory, passed away when I was pregnant with my second daughter. I think this was his way of letting me know he and my son Jamie are thinking of us three, here on Earth, while they are watching us from up above."

When I read Christina's story I could feel her excitement building as she found that last penny and freaked out with awe. What a special experience to have. That certainly feels like a direct conversation. One sure to never be forgotten!

In addition to the reassurance that we are not alone that many of us long for, there's another type of reassurance that most of us find ourselves looking for during our lifetime. The coins can help with that, too. Financial reassurance is up next.

## Chapter 5

# ♦ Financial Reassurance

The Message

If you find coins during a time of financial insecurity, these messages may be for you:

*Your prayers have been heard and are acknowledged. You are free to release any related worries.*

*You are not going through this period alone. Allow yourself to be at peace so that you're available for the resolution.*

*Return to faith. Remember that your Creator is unlimited, capable of endless miracles. Things can change in an instant.*

*You needn't spend your energy figuring out the "how" of the solution. Please let any obsessive thoughts go so that you're more available to pay attention to the world around you. Answers often come from unexpected sources.*

*Listen more carefully now when others speak. Their words or experience may serve as a divine spark, igniting the creative idea that brings resolution.*

Finding money when you're worried about money, during times of financial insecurity, is a form of reassurance. It's a sign that your concerns have been duly noted by the Divine. Consider the coin your invitation to breathe a sigh of relief and release the constant worry. This action creates the space necessary for divine help to reach you. By choosing to return to faith, you allow the Creator to use the Universe to provide.

Going back to the words of my guides about "opening energetic pathways," what we align with, for example worry and fear about money, is what we are creating an energetic pathway for. That pathway seeks to deliver to us matching energy — so more of the same.

If we choose to trust that the coin we found has significant meaning and allow ourselves to move into faith, we're aligning ourselves with the energy of receiving, thereby opening our energetic pathway to receive.

After all, didn't we just receive a piece of money? Just considering that more may be on the way is helpful.

Because I truly understand how difficult it can be to shed fear in trade for a more hopeful outlook, it feels right to take a quick diversion from coin talk to share a little process I have used personally. That doesn't mean I do it perfectly, mind you. But, when

I do, it's a big relief. My hope is that you may find it helpful, too.

## Spiritual Insight: Shifting Negative Viewpoints

When I find myself taken over by a negative viewpoint, I've strayed from looking at my situation with peace and hope. I've bought into the misery and abandoned the idea that some blessings first show up "in disguise."

For example: While exhausted, yet actively trying to heal a chronic illness, the roof in my apartment began to leak, which led to the discovery that the apartment had high mold counts making it necessary to move immediately. The situation was made extra stressful and complicated by an apartment manager who was a bully.

There were many invitations to submerse myself in fear. There were fears to indulge in beyond the money aspect, but since we're talking about money—money was a major concern.

Where could I afford to live? How would I pay for a move? Where would the new security deposit come from? What about all my stuff? How could I afford to replace what I now had to throw away? How would I pay for the specialty treatments to heal from mold exposure?

When my thought process has become stuck in the mire of fear, in order to find relief, I need to find a peaceful and positive thought pattern to replace it with. For me to actively shift, **I need to find a new viewpoint that makes as much sense to me as my fear thought pattern.**

This isn't about me puffing myself up with a bogus pep talk. This is about investing effort into finding a better perspective to believe in so I can find the peace within that will allow for a solution to be revealed.

How do I do this?

Imagine my mind as a Rubik's cube. When I'm troubled by fear, the color pattern of the cube has been twisted into a random mess.

As I try on new thoughts it's as though I'm turning the colors of the cube this way, or that way, seeking harmony through the alignment of all the colors.

I ask myself: Does this perspective give me peace?

If the answer is no, I keep clicking until I find the thought that brings all the colors back to alignment again and allows fear to leave. I will keep seeking until all the colors line up and I feel a shift within me.

There are times I'm able to find the peaceful

thought through praying to God, or my heavenly guides, with God's permission, step in and provide insight.

There are also times when I simply can't get the colors of the cube lined back up. If no guidance is forthcoming, I seek the counsel of wise and rational mentors, counselors, or drama-free friends.

The counsel you seek is a very important decision. There are those who love drama more than they love solutions. Real solution-seeking involves entrusting yourself to the person who can help you rise above.

I welcome the words, "Have you thought about it like this?"

When a trusted friend offers me a perspective I hadn't thought of, one that makes sense to me, I know I'm about to be set free.

In the case of moving from the moldy apartment, throughout the process when I felt overwhelmed, I re-centered myself with viewpoints I knew would help me get through it. To fend off fear, I created a list of positive potentials and chose to believe them:

- o It was a huge blessing to find out about the mold.

- o Could a move also be a blessing? A move opens up many possibilities. It was entirely possible that I'd end up somewhere much better, a place where true healing could occur; somewhere the maintenance staff maintained the property well and the manager was kind and reasonable. What a relief that would be!

o It was possible that living in a new place could change my life. It was entirely possible that I didn't need to fear "choosing the wrong place" but instead could trust that if I were to pay close attention, I'd notice that something higher was guiding me to the right apartment. I could trust that I would know my new home when I felt it.

o Once I was no longer living with mold affecting me daily, I may even get enough brain power back to write again. How healing and wondrous would that be?

## *Michelle's Story: When God Winks*

Many years ago, my friend Michelle and I were chatting about finding coins and "the signs" in life. I shared with her the unique things that had been happening to me around the finding of change and that prompted her to share a special dime story with me.

Long before our conversation, Michelle had noticed a pattern in her own life around finding dimes. She'd started to call the dimes "God winks."

This is what she told me:

"I always find dimes in the strangest places. They seem to show up in times of financial hardship, when I'm depressed over lack of money. I have many examples.

A few months ago, I was at the grocery store and didn't have a lot of cash. I stood at the check stand, digging around in the bottom of my purse for enough change to pay for my little bag of groceries and ended up spending all the money I had.

As I walked out of the store, I was telling myself that I spent my last dime on groceries. Literally.

When I got to my car, I opened the passenger door to load the bags and saw something shiny in the bushes next to where I parked. So I walked over to take a closer look.

Resting on top of a leaf was one shiny dime. You couldn't have balanced a dime on the leaf if you tried!

I picked that dime up and thanked God for it. Each time I find a dime, I interpret its message as: **Do not worry about money or finances. I will take care of your needs.**

There was also another day when I remember feeling depressed over finances, with no money to spend. I wished that I could buy something to cheer myself up. It was then that I remembered I had a Macy's gift card, so I went to look for it in the glove compartment of my car where it had been for months.

When I pulled the envelope out to see how much money was on the card, three dimes fell out of it and landed in my lap. How had they got in the envelope? I have no idea.

What are the odds of three dimes getting into that envelope? I had to chuckle. Then I sat in my car and thanked God for what I have in my life and for always providing."

Michelle told her sister about how often she was finding dimes and soon her sister was finding them all the time, too.

Michelle's story highlights what I've found to be true: Our own coin-related communication can begin simply because we believe in someone else's story.

On the face of it, change falling out of a gift card may not seem that momentous. A skeptic might explain it away by noting that it was in her glove box. Sometimes people throw change in there.

In Michelle's case, however, significance lies in what is clearly ongoing communication. For one, it's always dimes. Two, they are always found around a money concern. Three, it's happened so many times now that it's just plain amusing. Four, it's become contagious.

## Lorraine's Story: Financial Reassurance

I'm grateful to share this story that comes from Lorraine Lopez, who describes herself as a wife and mother of three.

"Although I am a strong person, my financial concerns were getting the better of me. I've been feeling alone, even wondering if my guardian angel is gone.

One day I went to bed and started to cry while praying to Jesus and God. I dozed off while doing this. In a half-asleep state I heard pocket change jingle and saw a shadow go across my room. Assuming it was my husband, I went back to sleep. When he came in much later and I woke to kiss him goodnight, I realized it hadn't been him after all.

The next day I started to make the bed. There at the foot of my bed was a penny with a dime stacked on top. I felt like my guardian angel was back and letting me know not to worry.

Three weeks later, I folded my pajamas and placed them at the foot of my bed like I always do. Then I took my son to the bus stop, came back and went to make the bed.

There next to my pajamas was a single nickel. I stood there with the biggest goosebumps ever.

This continued for a couple months. I would find nickels in the strangest places around the house. My goosebumps turned into smiles. I felt the comfort I needed every time I found one."

Not only does Lorraine's story give hope that finances will improve, but it also provides the deeply comforting reminder that we are not alone.

## April's Story: God's Special Communication

April was a twenty-year-old student at the time she wrote to me to share her experience with God and coins.

"It so nice to know that I'm not the only one out there who has been finding coins everywhere!

Most of the coins I find are pennies. This has been happening to me on and off for a few years now. I find them a lot in school and yesterday I walked into one of my classes and found four pennies right on my desk. I was amazed!

I always think of God when I receive them so I figure they are from Him. I feel like we have a special communication through these pennies.

One time, I found a penny on the ground when I was stressed over finances and took it to mean that it was God saying He would handle everything."

It warms my heart that at such a young age, April has already come to trust that she's receiving special communication from the Divine and understands how to apply it in a way that brings her peace and reassurance.

## *In God We Trust*

Perhaps the belief that finding coins is related to financial reassurance comes from the references to God on money itself, especially coins. In the United States, we have a long history of having the motto *In God We Trust* stamped on our coins. A quick Google search confirms that references to God also appear, or have appeared, on other forms of money around the world, like Canadian, Dutch, Nicaraguan, and British coins.

British coins bear the engraving D.G.REG.F.D which refer to the Latin words *Dei gratia Regina fidei defensor*, which means, "By the grace of God, Queen, defender of the faith."

As the message at the beginning of the chapter encourages, in order to receive help, it's beneficial to be in a state of faith. Coins that refer to God seem like the perfect reminder to put our faith back into God.

## *Spiritual Insight: Limiting the Creator*

Say you've been finding change. Often. You believe that your financial concern will be addressed in some awe-inspiring way. It would be so very human of you to now launch into trying to figure out—where? Where is this money going to come from?

I get it. I'm an answer girl, who is very familiar with the "maybe" game. Do you know this game?

Maybe I'll get a random check in the mail?

Maybe someone will give me a gift of money?

Maybe that metallic purple painted lamp will finally sell on Craigslist?

Maybe I should go online and check out the unclaimed money site?

Maybe I should play the lottery?

That's where the bottom part of the message at the beginning of the chapter comes in:

*You needn't spend your energy figuring out the "how" of the solution. Please let any obsessive thoughts go so that you're more available to pay attention to the world around you. Answers often come from unexpected sources.*

We are meant to let this aspect of things go. In other words, rather than try to lead, we follow the inspiration that comes to us. To lead is to continue the obsession by constantly trying to come up with all the different ways we may come into money. After all, can we really come up with what our Creator's options are using our limited human mind?

Try as I have, I've yet to figure out how to produce a miracle, but miracles from the Divine are actually pretty common.

If I can catch myself when I start spinning on the details, that's a good time to remind myself to "let go and let God."

There's a lot of peace in the thought that **our Creator is unlimited, with the power to change conditions overnight.**

## *Financial Affirmation*

If you're not fearfully obsessed with money, but just so happen to find change in a unique way while you're thinking about your future plans and money, that's very likely an affirmation that things will go well or that money is on the way.

## Chapter 6

# Creating Space
## ✧ for the Wonder of Life

In this section, there are multiple circumstances that call for a Message of Wonder because so many of us need to rediscover what is magical about life. And, every last one of us can benefit from experiencing the energy of wonder that opens, expands, and heals.

## *Messages for:*
### *Those Experiencing Chronic Illness*

If you are experiencing chronic illness and begin to find coins in very special ways and you're feeling "touched" by your findings, please consider these messages:

*You are loved and are being supported by those in the realm of the Divine. Immerse yourself in the nurture of wonder when you have these unique experiences.*

*Wonder is a lifeline during a time of illness. Keep your eyes wide open. Seek it. Invite it into your life and use its energy to keep your hope afloat.*

*Wonder reminds us that anything is possible. You are being asked to shift your thoughts away from illness and into possibility. Think about the unlimited potential of your Creator. A coin appearing where no coin could possibly be is a little miracle in itself. It serves to increase your awareness of miracles.*

## Messages for:
## The Uninspired, Bored or Disillusioned

If you're feeling uninspired, like life is too routine, or you're feeling disillusioned with life in general and you come across coins in the most extraordinary ways or places, check out these messages. One or all may be for you:

*You are being invited to re-discover the value of wonder, the inspiration it offers and its healing benefits.*

*Stop in the moment you find a coin and really allow yourself to soak in the magic of the experience. Lean into the reassurance that you aren't alone. You are watched over and you are understood.*

*You are being encouraged to create space for more joy and fun in your life by seeking what is uplifting to you.*

*Your guides and angels are willing to help you bring more wonder into your life and await your invitation for them to do so.*

*Your spirit longs for you to do more of what you love and to spend more time in nature.*

## Messages for:
## The Super Logical,
## Science-Minded, or Skeptical

If you're super logical, science-minded, or skeptical by nature, my guess is that you're not likely to be impressed by one little spark of wonder, say a single penny in a weird spot.

For you to notice that you're being courted by wonder, you're probably going to need a stream of coins, found in the oddest circumstances, with no reasonable explanation.

If that's you, I invite you to try on these messages. One or all may hit home for you:

*You are being invited to re-discover the value of wonder and to enjoy the freedom of accepting what is without explanation.*

*There's more to the experience of life than the human brain can process. You are being encouraged to open yourself up to experience life more through your sense of feeling.*

*When in need of answers, consider sitting still and allowing yourself to feel or sense what you need to know rather than "thinking on things." You may find that the wisdom offered by your body and heart is far more fulfilling than the wisdom of the thinking mind.*

*You are being encouraged to create space for more joy and fun in your life.*

## *The odd, yet interesting experience is meant to interrupt the disposition of a mind very set in its ways.*

Some of us have mental filters in place that cause us to see the world through the eyes of hard logic — *Just give me the facts and nothing but the facts.*

There are those who filter their view of the world through their scientific data minds — *Prove it.*

Some of us use skepticism — *I see you trying to prove it, but good luck trying to convince me.*

And then there are others still with filters from long periods of difficulty, their views now shaded by disillusionment or illness.

You'll find no judgment here because I've walked in those shoes. What I've learned about these filters through being broken open by cognitive challenges is that narrow ranges in thought patterns like black or white, right or wrong, good or bad—the kind that don't allow for grey areas—crowd out the nurturing energies of joy and wonder.

Without joy and wonder to offset stress, logic, science, or skepticism, life becomes out of balance. Humans need wonder and joy to feel fulfilled.

If we have become uninspired, disenchanted with life, or have been ill for way too long, we desperately need the nurture and restoration of spirit that wonder can offer.

For those who have been feeling uptight or super stressed, the body is constricted when in protective mode. If we become dazzled or feel awe, we suspend the energetic clampdown that stress has created. Wonder benefits us by opening our energy up. Whether it lasts a few moments or all day, it's good for the body to have a break from restriction and enjoy a period of free flow.

## What Can Wonder Do for You?

Let me give it to you straight: Wonder is one of the highest vibrations—alive and sparkling with the essence of our Creator.

Wonder is sustenance for the spirit—a beneficial, life-enhancing energy that can stimulate a will to live, provide meaning to life, uplift, and transform. It's the stuff that miracles are made of.

Throw your arms open wide to wonder. Within its energetic embrace, wonder wraps you in hope, healing, inspiration, awe and curiosity—all positive, life-affirming energies.

If you look up the definition of wonder, inside its word family you will find other high vibration types like: marvel, phenomenon, awesome, miraculous, admiration, reverence, and fascination. This is the energy you want to bathe yourself in every chance you get.

I speak to you from my heart, from experience. As a woman who has felt close to death many times during a chronic illness, it was the moments of wonder reaching into my soul that offered me hope and possibility, strengthening my will to live.

## *Spiritual Insight:*
## *Enlarging the Wonder Gateway*

Do you want a life that's more interesting, fun, and meaningful? The framework for this life is already in place around you. Your invitation to a divinely connected and wonder-filled life show up every day in the form of synchronicities and the interesting, yet unexplainable happenings in your life.

*Every coin you find is more than just an invitation to a divine conversation. It's also a gift of wonder.*

Pennies, quarters, dimes, and nickels make great messengers and contributors of wonder. Bear in mind, though, that coins are just one inlet in the river of divine communication. It's good practice to stay open to all wonder offerings because when I say wonder is "connected to coins," I'm not saying coin wonder is better than other forms, or that it's limited to them. Every glorious *wow* life throws at you is your chance to bask in the glow of wonder.

In addition, there's a gentle stream of wonder trickling into your life each day in more subtle ways. Look around you. Take it in. There are breathtaking sunsets, stunningly beautiful flowers, double rainbows, cool cloud formations, and leaves that long to be watched as they gently rustle in the wind. Nature lives to serve you wonder.

Moments of wonder here and there, enjoyed and felt within your heart, call out through the energetic pathway, "Insert more wonder here." Appreciation of these precious moments are your "investments" in expanding the wonder gateway.

If a noteworthy pattern has developed and the other messages in the book don't feel like a fit, you're probably being blessed by "wonder intervention." The question the coins beg you to ask is: Have I become disconnected from the wonder of life?

I had many years' worth of experience creating "wonder blocks" in my own life. And no clue that I was doing it. My moments of wonder or joy were fleeting, usually showing up connected to business inspiration, or me somehow getting a material possession I wanted.

As an adult, it's easy to forget what's enchanting about life. I need only look back to the year 2006 to find myself caught up in a whirlwind, completely detached from the rest of the world. After all that's happened since, I've had plenty of time to figure out how I became so out of balance.

After self-review, this is what I found to block the wonder in my life:

- o I was overly identified with my mind, routinely ignoring any wisdom my body offered me.

- I was pre-occupied with my thoughts. I obsessively thought, thought, and thought more about everything, which cluttered my mind with unhelpful, unproductive thought forms.

- I was a detail-oriented data brain. Type A all the way. Obsessed with reason and logic. My life was about goals, goals, goals. Work. Work. Work.

- Due to lack of self-worth, I was also chronic about giving myself away and being a people pleaser.

- I didn't know how to love or honor myself, so a lot of my choices were self-abusive.

Did I ever have good days or enjoy myself? Sure, I did. But I was even known to make work of that by trying to create the right conditions for fun to flourish.

My nature was to force the stars to align, therefore there weren't a lot of chances for wonder to happen organically. I wasn't present enough to notice that good stuff also happens on its own, outside of my design.

The overall feeling of daily life was less than wonderful. Mostly, life felt like a black-and-white photo, void of the divine texture that makes life so abounding in sensation and vibrant color. I was unfulfilled, so disconnected from the wonder of life that I almost needed a piano to fall in front of me to notice that something significant had happened.

What I've learned is that guidance from above is always present. No falling pianos are necessary.

The messages arrive in many forms; they are often not dramatic and it is totally possible to reconnect to the vibrancy of life by noticing the unusual placement of a few coins. They carry with them energy that supports transition.

IF...you are in.

Are you in?

Now, if you're feeling quite intrigued by a singular incident around a coin, maybe you don't need an intervention. But I'd say you still got a playful nudge from your Creator to have some fun and enjoy the wonder of your own existence in this beautiful world.

Finding coins in unlikely ways, like in a spot that you're certain was empty when you last left it, inside your already made up bed, or in the shoes you've been wearing for two hours—these little incidents are shots of mystical fun. They serve as reminders, or wake-up calls, that in this phenomenal world of ours anything is possible.

I mean, come on, sometimes coins even arrive out of thin air!

As one person shared with me:

"I was sitting at my desk working out my finances, feeling concerned over the credit card debt I have, when I heard a coin land on the floor, right by my foot. It came from nowhere."

And another:

"I was sitting on my sofa when, out of nowhere, a penny came rolling across my hardwood floor. I watched it roll for a while before it circled and came in my direction."

And another:

"One night when I was working late a dime came from above me and dropped onto my desk...Another time a dime came out of thin air and dropped in front of me while I was getting dressed. I find dimes everywhere in the strangest places..."

The mystery and fun of things that are unexplainable—this is the magic of life. When we're young, we don't dissect it. We embrace the magic and simply enjoy it. As we grow up, some of us lose the ability to get lost in awe. Instead, we become overly-identified with our minds, egos, relationships, careers, and possessions. It's easy to get sucked into analyzing, preparing for what comes next, or trying to control outcomes.

Not everything is meant to be categorized, thoroughly understood or scientifically document- ed. When something happens that defies your logic, as a human, you're naturally programmed to open yourself up, for however short a period, while you seek an explanation.

If the occurrence is "far out" and unique enough, you may even find yourself willing to broaden your current beliefs. Perhaps there's more to this life than you previously thought?

If you relate to the descriptions in this section, I hope you will pick up the coins you find and pay attention to the circumstances. It wasn't until I started picking up every random coin that crossed my path that I began to see a pattern.

Just for fun, why not consider each coin an invitation to the Wonder Party?

To get to the party, you have to walk through the grey area of life first, allowing it to expand your perception beyond black and white. The grey area is the place right before you get to an explosion of color and fun.

## Spiritual Insight:
## Wonder Is a Celebration for the Soul

The state of wonder is a celebration for the soul.

To experience wonder with increasing regularity is a sign of spiritual expansion and awakening. It's an affirmation that you're communicating with your soul, the part of you with access to the divine realm.

By placing your attention on what is wondrous about life, you nurture an intuitive conversation that, if honored, will enrich your life in the most delightful ways.

## Peter's Story:
## Wonder from the Bahamas

Peter Hardwick of New Hampshire wrote me to share this story. It's quite the head scratcher.

"I was kneeling down one night by my bed saying my prayers. When I finished, I got up and turned my covers down to get into bed. As I pulled the covers back, there was a ten-cent Bahamian coin sitting in the middle of my bed.

I have never been to the Bahamas or even to the Caribbean, which adds another twist to my story. I live alone and no one has entered my house in years.

I have been trying to figure out what meaning this coin has in my life. I would like to know because I'm completely baffled. I've asked friends and family and they tell me it is a blessing of some sort."

This situation provides a high level of intrigue since there's no way to explain a Bahamian coin. That's a pretty dazzling *wow* factor.

I wrote Peter back to tell him I believe a coin that turns up immediately following a prayer is a very positive sign. The image that comes to mind is a loving guardian angel offering a gift of reassurance to let Peter know that his prayers were heard and acknowledged.

## Story: Dimes for a Skeptic

A few years ago, I received an email from a woman who told me right up front that she was not a spiritual person. And not a spiritual seeker.

However, she had been finding dimes everywhere, for quite a while. She never found any other type of change; just dimes, dimes, and more dimes.

The spiritual part of her experience, as I see it, is that collectively, the incidents were powerful enough to rouse the wonder of a non-believer.

She was curious enough to go online and do a search about dimes, curious enough to email me and tell me her story.

Although she let me know that nothing on my blog had convinced her that there was meaning behind all that change she's finding, a self-described non-seeker was now seeking an answer.

That is meaningful!

I smiled when she told me in closing that she'd continue to look elsewhere for an answer. I celebrate the potential of where her curiosity may lead her because when there's no scientific answer to be found, one is left with just wonder...

## Christopher's Story: Opening the Door to Wonder

Christopher Enborg's story is compelling testimony of what can occur once a person begins to view the coin-finding process as divine communication.

"By the time the following incident occurred, I already had a couple months under my belt of redefining what it meant to find a coin. Previously, I was aware of the coins that crossed my path but my participation stopped at observation.

I told myself the coins I noticed were for someone more in need, a person who might pick them up to spend them. I never considered the Universe may be answering or acknowledging my financial concerns with a random penny.

Then I was introduced to the idea that coins could be some sort of communication. What? I'm worthy of that? I'm important enough for Spirit to take time to console me? These are some of the questions that swirled around in my head. This was the conditioning I was in the process of allowing to change when I entered a local grocery store.

On this particular day as I headed into the store, I guess I challenged the Universe, because I told myself that if I could find a penny in there, I would let it serve as validation that Spirit had noticed me after all.

As I made my way to the first aisle, my eyes scanned the floor, searching for "my penny." I then heard the thought, *"Why just a penny?"*

*What was that? Was I being challenged to set*

*my sights higher? Was it me asking this question,* I wondered, *or my divine friend?* Not knowing, I just kept walking.

A few seconds later I heard the suggestion to picture the coin I was looking for. So I pictured the next best thing to a penny—a nickel. But then, as if to challenge my decision, the voice came again—*"Just a nickel?"* So I progressed to a dime and heard the question raised again—*"Just a dime?"*

I answered this voice in my head with the thought, *"Ok, I get it. A quarter it is."* I understood the real challenge was to stop seeking the minimum when asking for divine intervention.

Let it be noted that I was making a conscious attempt to delay any sort of judgment of what I was doing. After all, I was adjusting my plan according to a voice in my head. And that voice was saying things I don't normally say to myself.

While sweeping the floor with my attention, I grabbed the items I needed and made it to the checkout stand. Sigh. I was now leaving and I'd found no coins whatsoever. I was more than a little disappointed.

I had a name for this type of

disappointment— Spiritual Abandonment. Years of this feeling had taught me to protect myself against the heartache of hope. So there at the checkout I began the process of letting go of the hope I'd had around finding a quarter and feeling connected to Spirit.

After paying for my items, I started to walk past the other checkouts to the furthest exit. Maybe I was hoping a little more time would help me find a quarter.

About halfway to the door I saw my daughter's ex-boyfriend walk in. He saw me and started to walk in my direction, so I did the same. We met close to the exit, about 5 feet away from the last checkout stand.

We talked and laughed, catching up on a few obligatory topics. As we approached our goodbyes I heard the sound of a coin drop near the checkout stand. Stopping mid-sentence I looked away from my friend and down to the floor until my eyes spotted a spinning silver coin. Then I looked up at the lady who I figured dropped it. Rather than pick it up, she just walked off.

The coin began to roll. My daughter's ex and I both watched until it staggered itself directly in front of me. It looked big. It was flashy. It made lots of noise. I kept watching until it stopped spinning and revealed what it was — a quarter.

*My quarter.*

Bending to pick it up, I acted like it was nothing and said goodbye. I had to get some space and process this. I realized I now had a choice to make — hold this experience in wonder or chalk it up to meaningless coincidence.

It felt deeper than that, like I also had the choice to honor and answer the original questions I had prior to this experience and make new decisions...

I am important. I do have worth. I can engage with the Divine and it will engage back. Who's to say if it was simply me talking to me in my own head or if that encouraging voice was something else? It doesn't matter. Because that day I walked away with a deeper sense of wonder and feeling a bit more connected, all because I chose to engage."

## *My Wonder Story: Instant Response*

Oh, how I enjoy a quick hello from Heaven and the playful reminder that I am watched over....and heard.

Years ago, back when I could still occasionally eat at select fast-food restaurants, my mom and I got hungry while running errands. I pulled into *In and Out Burger* and parked.

Out of the blue I said to her, "It's been a really long time since I found any change. Have you found any lately?"

"Nope," she said, as she shook her head.

We walked toward the entrance with me leading her through the rows of parked cars. Once we came into the clear, I looked down. Coins were scattered in front of me on the black asphalt so I stooped to pick them up.

My mom and I started laughing out loud. A penny. A dime. A nickel. And a quarter. One of each? Well, that was a first.

A gentleman standing by the entrance door smiled at us and said, "Just a minute or so ago a young girl came out through here and tossed those up into the air."

I looked around. What young girl? I hadn't seen any young girls while walking in.

At the same time I was telling my mom, "It's been awhile since I found change," a young girl was tossing her change into the air for me to find.

How fun is that?

And, what are the odds, I wonder?

## Chapter 7

# Coin Intervention:
## ✧ A Living Life Review

The message in this chapter is in a category all its own. The prompting of a life review glistens with potential.

The Message

If you begin to find coins every single day, almost everywhere you go, and this lasts for a significant period of time, like a couple weeks or a month, and the coin finding becomes impossible to ignore, filling you with a sense that something is really trying to get your attention, it's very likely that this message is for you:

*You are being encouraged to do a life review. The time is right to balance and harmonize your life. Energetic support is in place to help you make healthy change.*

(The method I use for life review is included at the end of the chapter.)

This is where the journey with coins began for me. I received a "coin intervention" during a time when I was so lost that I truly believed I was on track. The encouragement to review and realign my life was a call to save my life, not that I knew it at the time. That full story would require its own book. So what I'm sharing in this chapter is the spiritual insight that was part of my wakeup call. It's relevant for many who may read this. I'm also sharing my story, the first experience with coins that awakened me to this type of communication.

I'm the kind of girl who can get really caught up in life. When we are caught up in the business of life, our awareness isn't always on point, which is why the messenger coins in this category have a more dramatic strategy to get your attention. They will bombard you.

Imagine your heavenly guidance team pre-scattering coins in the areas you're expected to go and the coins waiting with excitement for you to show up and find them.

When I received my wakeup call, the pennies arrived every single day for approximately six weeks, which really amped up the *whoa* factor.

Since then there have been other short, intense, coin-abundant periods that lasted a couple weeks or so. This is when I find change anywhere I go, almost every time I leave the house, usually multiple coins in one day. I've gotten so in tune that I can get out of my car and "know" I'm going to find a coin. I can be walking toward a store and know there's a coin under the grey car I'm walking by. I can feel a coin, stop in my tracks, look around and find it. It's pretty wild.

If you find yourself experiencing this type of thing, you won't have to ask yourself, "Is this what she was talking about in the book?" These "pennies from Heaven" phases are really in-your-face noticeable.

Let's talk about what you may be invited to do. What's the point of a life review? The purpose is to help yourself become aware of the areas in life that need restoring to harmony. Since many of us are great at soldiering on, we may not notice that we've become out of alignment. We may overlook subtle feelings of disharmony within and choose to head down paths that aren't for our highest good.

There are many reasons a person could find themselves encouraged to do a life review and there are also different levels.

There are those who will receive a prompt from the coins that feels like a loving nudge to simply step back on track. Example: A young person begins to have a few smokes with their smoker friends. They are not yet addicted, but are on the threshold of developing a habit. At this point, they could simply stop, "get back on track" and avoid a related consequence.

The coins for another person may have to do with decisions they're in the process of making. A life review could reveal where they're operating unconsciously, rather than aligning with the guidance of their soul. Example: A person has lost a job doing work they dreaded. Rather than recognize that they now stand in the doorway of creation, rather than considering what other options they have, out of habit they begin to look for the same type of job that's always proven to be unfulfilling.

A review done by another set of folks may bring forth the knowledge that a much-needed lifestyle change is in order—that they're really off course and perhaps even bringing harm to themselves. I fell into this category.

In any event, no one is the worse for having checked in with their soul. The good news is that when these coins are affectionately staged all around you, heavenly back-up is already in place waiting to help you. YOU do, however, have to light the fire inside yourself first. In accordance with the Spiritual Law of Free Will, your divine team will need to feel your true intention to change, or hear your statement that you intend to change. Claim it out loud. "I'm ready to change my life and I accept the help of those the Creator would send!"

Before I share my story and the way I do a life review, I've been guided to speak to the most extreme call for a life review in the section of Spiritual Insight that's up next.

## *Spiritual Insight:*
### *Living Out of Balance*

Multiple coins found in the circumstances that follow are intended as a lifestyle intervention.

This goes out to those living extremely busy, overcommitted lives, those moving at warp speed, and those living *la vida* overwhelmed. These lifestyles fall into the category of risky behavior, although they are not usually recognized as such. In our culture, people who live this way are often admired and encouraged.

Yet, pushing yourself too hard can be hazardous to your health. I've been taught by my guides that constant activity, when perceived as stress by the body, may disrupt the electrical field of the body itself.

There's a window of time that a human body may sustain disruption before effects begin to show. Because of that delay—that blessed period when we have a chance to get back on track with minor consequences—we often don't recognize that cause and effect are at work behind the scenes.

Saying that consequences could be a matter of life or death should a person elect to stay off track is not dramatic.

If one is on a path to manifest a major spiritual lesson, the person will be offered gentle warnings along the way. Little indicators will flash around them and initially, they're easy to ignore.

Then, tolls begin. Tolls may be paid through error making, an increasingly woeful viewpoint, victim thinking, health "nuisances" like increased fatigue, regularly catching the latest bugs that go around, or forgetting things, etc. I'm not talking about one little thing. These types of tolls compound, but are often not noticed when a person's lifestyle is overly busy or rushed.

If one chooses to ignore the gentler warnings and the tolls, at some point life may be abruptly slowed to a crawl, creating the need for urgent re-evaluation.

If this happens to you and you find yourself in the uncomfortable spot of an imperative life review, you aren't being punished by your Creator.

You're probably off track and are now being invited to reconnect to your guidance system and re-evaluate your entire life so you may rebuild it upon what is truly meaningful.

When we are doing too much without enough

periods of "being," we stand to overwhelm our circuitry, which may drive a person's essence outside of their body. The old saying "I'm beside myself" is another way of stating that a person has become detached from their divine guidance system.

Our internal sensor is one of the most important things we have going for us. To live connected to this system is to live with a guide illuminating the safest, most beneficial path for your everyday life.

Our intuition and gut instinct help us sense and avoid danger. Our inner guidance reveals who is the most trustworthy among us and who we'd benefit from steering clear of. It's the source of helpful random impulses, like ideas to stop what we're doing and try something different.

The impulse may be a craving to eat something new because the new food contains nutrients your body needs to function optimally. It may also be the impulse to go into the office early today, an action that keeps you safe on the drive in.

Can you think of a time recently when you were too busy, felt scattered, or felt overwhelmed? Try to think back to what was going on in your mind at the time. Mental chaos I'm guessing?

Overwhelm can result from a mind running amuck without a divine guide, a mind flitting from this topic to that, offering vast amounts of input and random thoughts. While it's happening, it's almost impossible to comprehend all that's going on in there.

Moving from overwhelmed to shut down is not a lengthy process. If you find yourself shutting down, it's a coping mechanism; a blaring indicator that EXTREME NURTURE IS NEEDED TO RESTORE THIS HUMAN TO SAFE FUNCTIONING.

How many of us practice nurture, though? Please consider yourself invited to restore the practice of nurture in your life. You may benefit from pre-establishing a "nurture plan" so if you find yourself overwhelmed you don't need to figure it out then. What would it look like to launch into full nurture mode, recharge your batteries, and restore your brain to full function?

What would you need to do—or not do?

What's the "emergency" one-night nurture plan? The weekend-long nurture plan? You can do this. This is how you love yourself. There's a lot at stake.

When we allow ourselves to operate in a frazzled state, our guidance system has been abandoned in trade for another one. The super busy, out-of-touch-with-the-body person is a person under the influence of their mind and ego. And when the mind is allowed to dominate, it's like it gets drunk on itself. Yikes!

The angels brought up intoxication to me because the busy, overwhelmed state has characteristics in common with being "under the influence."

The risk of being in la-la land is that it's easy to miss things and make costly errors. When we are overwhelmed, we can still walk and talk, but our memory recorders may be faulty, the decision process, flawed. The overwhelmed are quicker to say, "Screw it!" when it comes to quality or attention to detail.

The temporary solution is in the nurture plan. A long-term solution may be found in a life review.

You may be wondering what any of this has to do with finding a stray quarter or dime. Here's your answer:

The loving hand of the Divine will reach out to those running on autopilot. The strange sight of a dime balancing on a leaf, like in the *When God Winks* story from the *Financial Reassurance* chapter, can also serve as a way to capture your attention and shift you to the present moment. Bring yourself present, my friend. Let us all bring ourselves present.

If a coin catches your attention when you're in a busy trance, I hope you'll stop, pick it up, and allow yourself to "have a moment." You've been blessed. It's very fortunate to receive the gift of being awakened from a haze in a GENTLE way.

## A side note about busy children and teenagers:

What a shame it would be for children to become too busy for wonder. After all, isn't that part of our purpose as children—to find wonder everywhere and remind the adults where it's at, too?

Aren't some kids these days overbooked with activities? This creates great stress on their young systems. Combined with the "normal" diet of eating void-of-nutrient food and constant electromagnetic fields (EMFs) flowing from personal electronics into their not-fully-developed minds and bodies, conditions are being created for our next generation to be frazzled before they even begin their adult years.

Just a little food for thought—offered with love.

## *My Story: Penny Intervention*

Up until this section you've been reading about people who find coins and understand the meaning of those coins. Now you're about to read the story of a person with no clue what the coins mean.

We're going back in time to the beginning of my coin-finding journey, back to when I was both dazzled and baffled.

I was clear on one thing only for weeks: Pennies were bombarding me. While I tried to sort out whether I was receiving a message of some kind, I was mostly amused with brief moments of frustration caused by not understanding what it all meant.

It took me weeks to process. The insight gleaned and written about here came later from reflection.

The experience was so wondrous and profound that it stayed with me, creating intrigue, which led to the opening of an energetic pathway, which led to conversations with others, which then led to me writing about it. It's the original catalyst, the reason I began to pay more attention to see if I could discern a pattern and learn what coin messengers might have to say.

The story is from 2010, an experientially rich year, though my participation in life was growing smaller by the minute. With fierce determination and a whole lot of denial, I was pushing as hard as a human could to carry on "normally."

My body was sounding a gong, but I didn't know how to listen to it. For the rest of my life, I will continue to make amends and seek ways to honor my amazing body and spirit.

My story is for those out there who may also need to start the process of reconnecting to their body and spirit with love. Societal conditioning, through which we've been taught to ignore ourselves rather than care for ourselves, needs reexamination. Many of us are missing the mark.

In addition to being "checked" by the Universe, through this experience I was blessed to learn that a flurry of coins could be divine communication. Thank you for teaching me that, God.

Here we go:

It was April 2010. I was forty-one years old. The joyful energy of writing and self-publishing my second book had created a "hope high" that I was now descending from. When my feet hit the ground again, I noticed two things: Sales from my first two books weren't likely to support me, and I wasn't feeling as healthy as I previously thought myself to be.

As mentioned in the introduction to this book, my brain had changed, leaving me unable to regularly do the work of my career or other normal income-producing work. I was offering angel readings out of my home by referral, as well as occasionally facilitating small meditation groups which I called Sacred Circles.

I'd been wrestling with a decision for weeks — should I try to grow my small spiritual practice by renting a room in an office?

It wasn't that I had much money to invest in this venture—I didn't—but I knew if it was meant to happen, the money would come. For now, I was simply doing research (opening an energetic pathway) into what type of space would work best when I was ready.

First up, I went to see a room inside an acupuncture office. Glass double doors opened from an angle into a golden-colored conference room. The size was perfect for an eight person Sacred Circle. But, I wondered, *how could a room so large be made cozy enough for one-on-one angel readings?*

My mind flashed to a vision of two oversized burgundy chairs placed facing each other on a thick gold rug in the back corner of the room. Two small bookcases sat behind the chairs. Soft light emanated from candlestick lamps on top of the bookcases. In instant response to my inner wondering, I was shown how to set it up with stuff I already owned.

The owner of the business, Sarah, was my age. Her energy filled the office with the serenity of a Japanese garden. We stood in her lobby area chatting like longtime girlfriends catching up on life. She was so easy to talk to I confessed that I'd never rented a space before. I was nervous about making a commitment even though the room was perfect for my needs.

Nodding her head in understanding, she smiled warmly and suggested a two-month trial run, giving me an irresistible rental price.

On the drive home, I thought about how I felt

like I'd known Sarah all my life. And what about that comment she made? "I was wondering when you were going to show up."

*What a strange thing to say*, I thought to myself, *unless, of course, Sarah was expecting her soul sister to come rent from her.*

I gave myself a few days to consider the room. Inside, I felt **no sense of urgency**, no attachment to an outcome, just the calm knowing that everything would be fine. With delight, I noted that inspiration for new Sacred Circles had began to trickle into my awareness. That was a good sign.

A check arrived in the mail. After opening it, I chuckled to myself. The amount was enough to pay the two months' rent. It was time to move in and give it a go.

How divine.

Once the room was set up, the trickle of inspiration gave way to a flood. Ideas for seminars, classes, and meditation CDs swooshed into my mind. I even heard new books starting to write themselves in there.

So many exciting ideas were coming at me that in self-defense, I decided to write them down. Rather than feel organized, the list made me feel disappointed, like there was so much I should be doing. Yet, I was so unbelievably tired. Who even knew that a person could be this tired?

For a woman with workaholic tendencies and concerns about how to support herself, this is where things get tricky. I didn't notice that the energy of flow had taken a sharp turn, right out of alignment and into the forceful nature of ego.

It was right around this time that the pennies began to show up.

As part of a daily routine, I walked the small community where I lived. The neighborhood consisted of a large circle with just one way in and out. In ten minutes, you could walk the whole outer edge of the circle unless you got to visiting with neighbors.

Up until this point in my life, coins on the street rarely caught my attention, but now each day on my walk I was noticing pennies. I'd been walking this same small area every day, sometimes twice a day, for years. There were a few coins here and there in the past. Nothing notable. But now, all of a sudden, there were too many pennies to ignore.

Amused, smiling to myself each time I found one, I made the decision to pick them up from now on. Surely they were heavenly high-fives celebrating all the cool things that were happening.

I remember feeling so certain I was headed down a divine path because everything had come together so beautifully. I could list every synchronicity, every captivating flash of the Creator.

Yet in the blink of an eye, I was seduced off a divine path and into oblivion by the pressure of a self-inflicted to-do list. Ego guidance found its entry point, took over, and started pushing angelic input out. And me? I had no clue that I'd gotten lost.

I was officially "off the divine guidance channel." Gentle whispers gave way to a louder, whip-cracking, bossy voice **with a sense of urgency.** This motivational speaker in my mind, although encouraging me to do loving things, was not coming from a place of love at all. It bullied me into sacrifice mode using the rallying cry, "A person in service to the Creator should be willing to do more and give it their all."

The inner chant? Chop. Chop. Do more. Try harder. Go faster.

How slick that darn ego guidance is. Using a positive goal, it captured my attention and then energized the workaholic part of my personality. That part of me has a history of mercilessly pushing past every bodily limit until consequences become dire.

(I'm about to include the lessons of insight I was given for myself at the time, by the angels.)

## Angel Insight One:
## Urgency Equals Ego

There's no rush in the Creator's world.
A sense of urgency implies that you
may miss out on, or lose something you're
supposed to have, rather than trusting what's
meant for you will always find you and
find a way to happen.

Fatigue had turned my limbs into heavy sandbags. Hoping that exercise may grant me access to the Well of Energy, I pushed to keep up my walks, overlooking the amount of times I needed to stop and force air deeper into my lungs. I wasn't overweight, or even that out of shape, yet I had trouble walking a leisurely pace for more than five minutes at a time.

It had sunk in by now that "something" was trying to get my attention. Why else would I still be finding pennies every single day on my walks?

What were the odds? It was so curious. Theoretically, after walking every day in a small circle for years, even if there had been an abundant supply that no one else ever picked up, wouldn't that be dried up by now? The coins were being replenished daily.

Whether I walked with others or walked alone, the penny was always there...somewhere.

I remember the day my mom came for a walk with me and we made a game out of it. Both of us hunted for the lucky penny. Guess what happened? We each found pennies that day. In front of the same house, no less. Too funny.

Fatigue or no fatigue, I was still excited by the new freedom to open my practice up further. I would hold weekly Sacred Circles for the two months of my trial run.

Coffee was my personal assistant, entrusted with the responsibility to keep me going through each class. There was something so special about hanging out in a group of likeminded souls doing spiritual growth exercises and meditating. Surely the coffee and the joy I felt from facilitating the circles would carry me for two hours.

A couple weeks into a Sacred Circle, near the end of the night, my mind went blank. Completely blank, like *What am I doing here?* blank. All eyes were on me. It appeared I'd been talking.

*Had someone asked me a question?* They were all still looking at me. I wondered how long I'd been sitting there. It was as if I'd visited another time/space dimension and returned sharply, without grace.

I also don't remember what happened until class ended, just that once it was over the room got LOUD. Everyone was talking at once, it seemed, through their own megaphone. It was quite jarring to the internal world of my brain.

The group was saying goodbye to each other, to me. I couldn't respond. No words would come. All I could do is smile and nod—staring at the others from inside a mental bubble.

I'd had plenty of strange brain things occur previously. What I didn't get at the time is that this "first appearance" marked a transition. The brain was entering a new phase; one that would make it possible for me to get lost inside the aisles of grocery stores.

Later that evening, one of the ladies in the group called to ask if I was all right. *Groan. She noticed.* I told her briefly what happened, then concluded that I needed to eat some almonds before class next week. Yes. Almonds and coffee. That ought to do it.

When I forced myself to walk that night it was getting dark. I made my way around the whole circle without finding any change. In the final stretch, just four houses from my home, I realized, *Wow. It's finally going to happen. There will be no pennies tonight.*

But right by my house, on the dark asphalt, there was a penny preparing to glisten as hard as it could through the twilight into my awareness. It succeeded.

Walks wouldn't be nearly as fun without this strange phenomenon. *But, dear God,* I prayed, *when am I going to find out what this all means?*

By then I'd done a good amount of angel readings from my home but because they'd been so sporadic, I really hadn't found my groove. I was still nervous before each one.

Looking back now, after living with a cognitive impairment for a long time, I can see that my lack of confidence was due, in large part, to an unrealized concern: *Will I be able to find the words to convey the guidance I receive?*

The challenge of converting the magnitude of divine guidance into limited human language is normal for intuitive readers. My challenge was greater because interpretation aside, I was already having trouble forming a sentence.

I wanted to ensure that I didn't disappoint a client so I would get into the zone for appointments by doing a long meditation beforehand. Stuff came through. Like a jump start, it helped boost my confidence.

Connecting to the angel realm, feeling the

unconditional love and acceptance, then sharing that insight with a client was euphoric for me during those days. The sensation of ethereal love enlivened me during a reading, helping me forget human fatigue.

Then it happened. Two different clients cancelled at the last minute. On two separate days, after I did a long meditation, showered, got ready, drove to the office and prepared the room, the client did not show up.

It felt like the end of the world.

Collapsing into the oversized chair, I closed my eyes. The lights were already dimmed. I was grounded by the fact that there would be no energetic high that usually helped me drive home.

Cancellations are an unfortunate part of regular business, yet the second time it happened I was irrationally upset. I rummaged through my thoughts, looking for the reason for such a high level of irritation. Thoughts came running at me hysterically. *They wasted my energy for nothing!*

In truth, my distress wasn't about the clients at all. I was the one hurting myself by doing more than I could afford to do. Did I see that at the time? Sadly, no.

## Angel Insight Two:
## Divine Guidance or Ego Guidance

*Divine guidance doesn't encourage the uplifting of others at the expense of spiritual, emotional, or physical drain to yourself.*

In my defense, I'd already been to my doctor of seventeen years. My bloodwork was normal. The same doctor who pleaded with me over the years to acknowledge workaholic tendencies, to take time off to rest, now actually suggested I see a counselor to figure out why I was "unmotivated to work."

Grrr. That bugged me. Did he just put me and "lack of motivation" in the same sentence? Yet, I had no explanation for how a total of 3-4 hours of interaction with people a week could deplete me to the level of wanting to crawl into bed for days.

And still.

Every single day.

Pennies and more pennies.

Although I found most of them in my neighborhood, I was now finding them elsewhere too, like outside my car door as soon as I parked or while running errands.

My interest and participation had grown. I was now playing with the coins by trying to predict where the next one might come from. Before I got out of my car wherever I was, I tried to guess whether I'd find one. Since I knew for sure I'd find one while walking in my 'hood, my game was to try and sense—in front of which house?

One day while out on my usual walk, I heard the words, "Cross the street," in my head. So I did. Crossing at an angle, I walked directly into a penny on the other side. I just stood there and laughed out loud.

Seriously, those are the days that make a person stop in awe and let it sink in—there is definitely something much bigger than us at work in this world. And our guides are some pretty amusing characters.

On that day, I prayed yet again, asking God to please help me understand. I also implored my guides to help me.

*Please...what am I missing? Why is this happening? What is it that I need to know?*

Life was more than just to-do lists, Circles and angel readings. I was also still pushing myself to attend support groups.

Almost overnight, I became awkward with a few friends in the group. Our conversations now felt fake and transparent. Their personal agendas shone as brightly as flashlights into my eyes. And I was equally inauthentic, by trying to "act normal."

Normal, I wasn't. My intuitive ability had taken on surprising new intensity and I was floundering like a little kid in the deep end without her floaties. Like it or not, I was noticing for the first time whether my friendships were healthy or not.

People were naked to me now. Not physically, but in their internal worlds. Below the surface of their smiles, I saw intentions and motivations, their buried wounds and the stories they tell themselves.

Ironic, since I couldn't see my own.

When I listened to others talk, a visual representing their energetic life tapestry would open up before me. Glistening strings in rainbow watercolors and silver floated from their bodies at different levels in the air. The strings connected to images or events from life experience and revealed how the residuals affected their present day.

The tapestry was alive and vibrating with insight into the unconscious influences responsible for their behavior patterns. It was all there to behold: the desire to be a better human, the strength of the ego, the light, the shadows, and the part seeking divine consciousness. It was a kaleidoscope of the human experience: complex, colorful, remarkable. Its depth was worthy of my reverence.

While overwhelming to integrate, for those of us on Team Love, a gift like this naturally leads to even more compassion. The ability to see into those around you grounds you in the understanding that we're all the same. The planet is populated by people who all carry hope, wishes, sadness, pain, the desire to be better, frustration over perceived faults, complaints about others, and at least a touch of indignation that flares while driving. We all hide parts of ourselves at times and secretly hope we're good enough— that we matter in this world.

My compassion for others had expanded, but so had the awareness that I must learn to give more compassionate care to myself.

With this gift too, came the realization that there are those at places on their soul's journey who choose to be inauthentic. I could now easily sense those around me who wished to consume my energy with little regard for me or my health. They brought up topics hoping the "intuitive" would give them a free reading or insight. There were also others who tried to cleanse themselves by purging every dark, painful thought or emotion they had through my empathic heart. There were some "takers" in my friendship pool.

### Angel Insight Three:
### Your Inner Circle

Part of your life mission is to ensure that
the people in your inner circle, those with
the most access to you, especially the ones
you touch, hug, sleep next to or have sex
with, be the people you wish to run toward,
not away from.

To be straight, this clarity was not about judgment of the takers. It was information to prompt a course correction necessary to support my health. I was encouraged by my divine tutors, for the sake of energy preservation and good mental health, to engage only in true, heart-centered, mutually supportive, authentic relationships. It would be best to distance myself from some people as soon as I could. Sigh.

Of course they were right. Disengaging would require effort though. I'd have to completely change some of my daily life activities and find new support groups. I didn't want to. I was way too tired for that.

From past experience with takers, I knew that they stand to flare up when losing energy donors. The last thing I needed was some fatiguing drama. It seemed easier to not rock the boat. What would I say to others when they asked about my sudden distance?

Then came the day I couldn't bring myself to offer the obligatory hugs to those I no longer honestly wished to hug. A health cost was being paid from forcing myself to act normal. This "small lie" was more uncomfortable than any fallout might be. It was creating disharmony within.

One of my favorite lessons from the angels is, "There's no such thing as a little amount of disharmony."

I was then shown that this new gift in awareness arrived as the counterbalance to my lifelong ability to see into the heart of others, to see their God light, even when they weren't acting heart-centered. (This is how I became friends with the takers to begin with. I was busy looking at their inner spark, rather than paying attention to their outer behavior.)

However unsettling its entry into my life was, the gift was a provider of balance. I would now have an opportunity to use both parts of the "I see into you" gift. The yin to the yang.

Would you believe that there was a dip in the number of coins I found once I made the decision to move away from toxic friendships? It was an affirmation. And yet, I was still finding enough to ask myself, *Is there something more that I have yet to figure out?*

Years prior, when the doors to my intuitive abilities blew wide open, I read a book by Doreen Virtue and learned of Archangel Jeremiel, whose specialty is assisting us in making an honest assessment of where we are in life. He can help us see with clarity and offer insight into the changes that will serve the highest good. This idea came to mind.

It was clearly time to sit for a life review.

I prayed, asking the Creator that Archangel Jeremiel help me sort out my next step. Then I sat down for meditation, willing to receive an honest appraisal of my life, a fresh perspective and a clear message for a new path.

It hadn't even been the full two months since I moved into Sarah's office. Although my mind (ego) tried to convince me that it was too soon to throw in the towel, in the meditation I asked if I should give up the space. This prompted me to visualize and try on how it would feel to move out and remain friends with Sarah. For good measure, I even threw in the idea of giving up doing angel readings and Sacred Circles.

The relief that moved through me was so soothing, so warm and comforting, there was no question what needed to be done. I readily accepted that the time had come for me to begin a different journey, one of learning how to honor myself, my needs and my health.

As sad as I was to leave her office, when I told Soul Sister Sarah that I must give up the space, she understood completely. This is what happens when you find your other soul group mates. They support what's best for you. In fact, our friendship grew and more reasons for why we came to meet each other were later revealed.

When I went for my next walk, I had a companion with me, a walking buddy who had previously witnessed my penny magnetism in all its glory.

This time, on a whim, we decided to leave the subdivision, taking a random route that brought us onto busy streets and through a grocery store parking lot. It was ambitious, a longer walk than I was used to with way more opportunities to find change.

About half way, I stopped and gave a little push to my companion's arm. "Hey, we've walked all this way and I haven't seen a single coin or penny!"

He rolled his eyes at me playfully. "Yeah. Some penny magnet you are."

We laughed and started walking again. Less than ten feet ahead of me, not in the middle, but actually on my side of the sidewalk, three pennies were lined up perfectly in a row.

I shrieked out loud when I saw them. To be honest, I was a bit freaked out. *What are the odds,* I wondered, *that mere seconds after noticing I hadn't found any, I came upon a line of three?*

Astonished, I just stood there staring down at the concrete. Goosebumps ran up and down my arms and legs. Many people believe there's significance in the number three. In my case, there was. As I gazed at those three pennies, I intuitively knew the message was different this time. They were no longer imploring me to wake up and get back on track.

I felt the positive rush of affirmation. In my gut, I knew I'd taken the right action. FINALLY!

Guess what happened next? That's right. The pennies stopped. Thank goodness I have some patient spiritual guides working with me.

## Spiritual Insight: Doing a Living Life Review

The main purpose of a living life review is to allow your soul to communicate freely without the judgment of ego. The idea is to allow information to be revealed, rather than censoring it or debating with it.

What I'm sharing with you in this section is the way I'd personally sit for a life review.

## The short version of a life review goes like this:

While sitting quietly, breathe deeply. In the practice of good spiritual hygiene, I'd ask the Creator to surround me with loving energy to assist me in the process. For example: Jesus and my guardian angels or spirit guides. I may also ask for Archangel Jeremiel who, as mentioned, is said to be helpful with life reviews.

Once I felt peaceful, I'd ask if there are any areas of life that need my care or attention. Trusting the answer that arrives, I'd ask the next question—*is there action I should take?* If you do this and get an impression of some type of action, it's important to suspend judgment in order to follow the impression through. Mentally visualize following the suggestion while paying close attention to how the body feels. As you move through the visualization, do you feel better?

If you do, you now have a direction to invest in. Consider opening that energetic pathway the guides speak about so often.

The underlying vibe of divine guidance is always love, nurture and restoration of honor. Life reviews have a way of bringing to light the ways we aren't acting with honor for ourselves or others.

Guidance that comes from deep within is not usually concerned with ease of metamorphosis or the comfort of status quo. It's about what's best for you regardless of how inconvenient it may be to transform your life.

Therefore, your resistance is natural. At the same time, if your gut has recognized truth in a life review, there's an inner knowing that life will FEEL SO MUCH BETTER after change has been made. That, my friend, is how you know that change is worth it. Keep that feeling close to your heart so you can use it to counter any fear that may come up.

Because let's face it, change takes courage. Rest assured though, if you choose to alter your life for the higher good, you won't go it alone. Like the message at the beginning of the *Life Review* chapter tells us, when we're prompted to do a life review, there's energetic support in place to assist us.

We access this nurturance using our free will. This means we make our choice clear through prayer. We request that our angels be empowered to guide the process and help us keep our hearts open. Lastly, we stay aware and make sure we are "allowing."

Allowing is so important because however beneficial change is, while we're walking through it, it won't feel normal or comfortable. Change and comfortable are two energies not likely to exist at the same time.

If we reframe the temporary feeling of

unsettledness as the perfect sign of progress and proof that we are closer to a new and improved life—wouldn't that feel so much better than viewing the transitory feeling as a negative thing?

In addition to being based in love, honor, and nurture, another test of true divine guidance is that it doesn't dishonor you or others or carry with it an unwelcome repercussion. For example, it's not likely that in a life review, under normal circumstances, you'd be encouraged to flip your boss the finger and walk out on a job— even if you visualized it and it felt amazing. Smile. That visual may simply represent how freeing it will feel to leave. In this case I'd pray to be infused with the diplomacy to exit the job gracefully.

## *Spiritual Insight:*
## *The "In-Depth" Living Life Review*

If you want to get more in depth and you haven't done this type of thing before, below are some questions you could use to help get into the groove. These deeper questions can be asked one at a time or as many as you are comfortable with. Please sift through them using your divine filter and discern which may be most beneficial to you.

The idea isn't to sit and try to "find what's wrong." A life review can be used to expand your gratitude and sense of what's good about your life, too! The idea is to make space for clear insight so you may evaluate your life impartially.

Clear sightedness is free of bias, with space for appreciation and simultaneous assessment of the ways we can improve ourselves. This is a love-based process. Stay in the love.

Here we go:

Sit quietly. Breathe deeply. Ask God to surround you with safe, loving beings of light like those mentioned in the short version of the life review: Jesus, guardian angels, spirit guides, or Archangel Jeremiel, who is known to be helpful with life reviews.

Bring your attention to your feet and imagine thick roots extending deep into Mother Earth, anchoring you to the ground.

Take stock of what's beautiful about your life; what is good and what feels loving.

Evaluate your daily activities. Where are they aligned with what matters most to you? Where could they use improvement?

Mentally walk yourself through the different areas of your life—relationships, work, health, etc. Do this while paying attention to the sensations in your body and while asking yourself questions like...

- What do I like about my life?

- What do I do effortlessly and with love?

- What feeling would I like to have more of?

- What can I do to increase that feeling?

- Where do I need more nurture? More balance?

- Is there anywhere I am losing energy?

- What areas of my life need more attention?

- What actions could I take to improve life overall?

- Are there conversations, if I had them, that could create a sense of freedom within me?

- Is there anything I can do that would help my spirit feel lighter?

- Would I benefit from anything about my life being adjusted or completely changed?

- Is there anything my soul wishes for me to know?

Finish by imagining your life as it would be after you had already put this information to use—having made any changes, after you've had any challenging conversations (that ended well), after adjusting any areas of resistance or energy drain, after increasing nurture, after heeding your soul's call.

Does that feel better? Does that feel worth making change?

Please sit with that feeling. Ask it to energize and empower you as you commit to putting change into action.

Now smile. The divine realm will celebrate with you as you make positive, healthy change. God loves you. You love you. Your heavenly entourage is ready to rock these changes with you.

## Chapter 8

# ✧ Coins of Affirmation

*I once had a question and asked God to give me an answer through the coins: heads for yes, tails for no. I ended up finding two pennies side by side. One heads and one tails. I was so mad. But I had to laugh. — April, student*

I chuckled when I read April's comment, because I've done the same thing—tried to get a yes or no answer from the coins.

Many times I've asked to find coins as guidance. Finding them on walks seemed to be pretty easy so I tried suggesting that perhaps God could send me a coin as a "yes" on my next walk. The asking, then receiving a coin in direct response to my question hasn't turned out to be a strong method of guidance for me.

Mind you, I do find plenty of coins that I call affirmations. They just don't arrive on my schedule, or at my request. Instead, they seem to show up at random, when the timing has been deemed right by the Divine. Like a little hint from the ethers, they seem to whisper: *Psst. You're headed the right way.*

Don't forget though, as illustrated by my penny story, an affirmation is not carte blanche, or a divine signature co-signing everything that follows because it's still pretty easy as humans to find ourselves off track. Instead, I'd consider an affirmation coin a little blessing of encouragement for the moment you're in.

Learning to recognize an affirmation is a bit of an art. The good news is that this form of guidance isn't reserved for a special few. It is, however, most accessible to those who are in touch with their abilities to feel and sense.

As ridiculous as this may sound, a lot of people have no idea how they feel. In fact, some of us are masters at dismissing our senses. I've done it. I know it well.

There are also folks who are masters at feeling A LOT, although the focus is tuning into how EVERYONE ELSE feels. Looking outward is a fantastic diversion, hypnotic even. When we don't pay attention to ourselves, we get to avoid the responsibility or need for action that may come with self-awareness. Lots of us are more comfortable taking action on behalf of someone other than ourselves.

All that comes with daily life really is enough to pull our awareness outside of our bodies rather than toward our inner senses. Therefore, we are again faced with a choice on whether we invest. Will you choose to make the effort to develop the skill of feeling/sensing and learning to stay connected to your body?

Perhaps I should mention the payoff.

The world is alive and scintillating with information for you. The signs and messages around you become much easier to perceive when you've developed greater sense awareness. If this interests you, there are a couple spiritual insights coming up to help you.

It's no surprise that the process starts with intention, right? When you say to yourself, to your Maker, and your heavenly guides that you intend to recognize the affirmations offered to you as guidance through coins and to apply that guidance for the highest good, you're once again opening an energetic pathway to support your intention. Now that you're in your intention, how will you know if the coin you found was an affirmation?

First, ask yourself the question: What was I thinking about when I found it? If your thoughts were centered around an action, the coin may be a positive affirmation for you.

The message could be as simple as: **We hear you and like what you are considering.**

(I hear "we" when it comes to affirmations. My understanding is that the "we" is a collective of angels and/or guides.)

That's the first layer.

The second layer is energetic. The coin that serves as an affirmation carries with it the energy of positivity to encourage you. There will be an inner knowing that feels like a "yes" reverberating within you. It may give you the sensation of your heart expanding with warmth and joy.

Can you work with one coin as an affirmation? In the right circumstances, sure. But I wouldn't be the one to tell you what that looks like for you. For myself personally, even with a good amount of experience working with coins, when it comes to affirmations, I like to be certain. I want to experience an abundance of them before I make a move.

## The Affirmation Zone

If I could communicate with the coins that wish to affirm me, my request of them would be something like this: Please rain down and create a whole zone of "yes" energy for me to immerse myself in. Please provide me with a multi-layered, enchanting chain of events that feels like Heaven just reached down to high-five me.

That's what I'm looking for in my affirmations.

You see, accepting one coin for encouragement to take some sort of action makes me feel like I'm making up a reason to do what I want.

How will you know when you're in the zone? Coins will show up, though usually not alone. Other signs and synchronicities collaborate with the coins as though the Universe understands that we all long for a feeling of surety, which one little old coin may not provide.

For affirmations to feel legit to me, I prefer they show up in a very short timeframe and come in at least three events. I'm not saying this is the only way it can happen. I'm just sharing what feels comfortable to me.

If you think back to my penny story in the last chapter, the last thing that happened before the penny messengers faded into the background of life was that I found three pennies lined up perfectly in a row. This came after I made the much-needed course correction in my life.

The day I came upon them I was "in my knowing" that they were there to reassure me, to affirm that I did the right thing by choosing to honor myself and change my life. I could absolutely feel it.

Those three pennies were accompanied by another sense layer—goosebumps and an out-of-this-world feeling of awe.

Lastly, there was the added confirmation that I'd received all the guidance that was forthcoming at that time, when the phenomenon of finding pennies everywhere, every day, stopped just as abruptly as it had begun.

Please let me be direct here. If you find a coin after having the random thought that you should sell everything and move to another country, I wouldn't be too hasty to get on that. Discernment is your friend. Please use it wisely.

## *Spiritual Insight:*
## *A Look into the Affirmation Zone*

What follows is a story about my own experience with coins as affirmations. It's from an old post I wrote for my blog. The story showcases how other clues, synchronicities, and signs come together in harmony with the coins to offer a full melody of affirmation. It's a perfect example of how a chain of affirmations create the "zone" I'm looking for.

Here's the post from back in June of 2013:

"Today I'm posting to share my most recent story about finding change and how I accepted it as an affirmation of the guidance I'd received.

My Loving Source knows I interpret finding coins as communication. It's become part of our ongoing conversation.

How do I know that this conversation is with the Source of Light? Because when it happens, it feels like love. I'm often totally amused. When God winks, I giggle and answer out loud, "I see you."

Recently I did a blog post about what's going on behind the scenes of a person experiencing chronic illness. When the idea to do so first arrived, I was resistant. If it was something I was supposed to do, I knew the idea would gain momentum on its own.

I tried to ignore the inspiration. There were thoughts of protest. *What's the point of writing about illness at all? What am I going to do? Give a manifesto of my current complaints? Do I even have anything to share that might help others? I'm still learning to maneuver the ebbs and flows of this part of the journey; what could I possibly have of value to share?*

I could see me running into someone I know after they read my "true life" story. Would their faces show me that all they can see in me is illness? No, thank you. That would not be healthy for me. **Please do me the favor of seeing me as whole and healed.**

I considered my super-slick ego. I listened as it informed me that if I tell the world and accept help from others, when I run into someone I know in public, in order to justify that help, I would need to make sure they can tell I'm sick.

So, ego, just to clarify…what you're telling me is that I need to be sure and ACT SICK because that would be expected of me now?

What if I'm having a good day? I NEED to claim every single second of feeling good that I can. That's how a person heals. If I'm so tired today that I can't bring myself to shower but wake up tomorrow feeling rested and pain free, I need to turn the music up, dance around and embrace a *woohoo*! kind of day.

It's not only that my ego could tell me to "act sick because it's expected of me." That same darn ego is responsible for me also "acting just fine" when I feel like crap. We are taught to "act" one way or another.

My personal goal, however, is to be in touch with my body, authentic in the moment, allowing each moment to be whatever it is. It's a good idea for me to monitor myself for any "act" by continually asking: How do I really feel right now?

Another protest to God had to do with the whole attention thing. Yes, I do lay it all out on the blog so you may be shocked to know that I strongly dislike calling attention to myself and only "go all transparent on you" when I'm compelled by The Force to do so.

With concerns in mind, I began a conversation with my Maker: *Do you really want me to write about this? I don't know why. I don't know how. I don't see the point.*

That night I walked into my bedroom holding a binder in my hand. I decided, quite randomly, to put the binder on the very bottom of a bookshelf which is tucked behind a dresser in the corner of the room. There were much easier places to set the binder down. The position I had to get into was uncomfortable. Right in the space I was trying to shove the binder was a bright, shiny penny.

I smiled. *Okay,* I told God. *That was cute, but if you want me to really take this idea seriously, I'm going to need more.*

Soon thereafter, ideas and instruction began to arrive in my awareness, giving me the further prompt to move forward. I still felt resistant. *But my brain hurts,* I whimpered.

Creating a blog post, figuring out my website yet again—it was overwhelming! Because I have difficulty at times retaining what I've learned, each new blog post requires me to figure it all out again. There's a word for that. Tedious. I loathe tedious.

*Okay, okay, God,* I said. *I'll try.*

Going into home office area the next morning, I sat at the computer with very little expectation of myself. I hadn't been able to write in months. On this day, to my great surprise I was easily able to write. As the post took form, I started to see that it was more than just what may be perceived as whining. *Whew.*

I paused to take my amazement in. I could hardly believe that I was writing coherently! I took a deep breath to connect to the joy of this feeling, looked around the room and then down at the floor. Right next to my foot was a shiny quarter. *Hmmm. Where did that come from?* Combined with the way the post was flowing, the quarter felt like an affirmation that I was doing the right thing.

At one point I got up to do some laundry. As I picked up a load to put into the wash, change fell out. That was three coin events in less than twenty-four hours and I hadn't even left the house!

I finished writing early in the day. Once I write a post, I usually let it go for a day or so, so it can talk to me and tell me if it needs to be fixed in any way. On this day, I walked away from it intending to do the same. Soon I found myself crying. I was scared. I was about to put my heart out there and risk finding out if no one cared.

This gave me an opportunity to sit with the fear and ask it to show me where it came from. The thread of this fear—*how I feel doesn't matter*—led back to the five-year-old me. That five-year-old learned to keep quiet about her feelings and what she was going through rather than bother anyone

144

with her problems.

It didn't take me long to see this clearly so I got a little excited. Maybe this was why I'd been guided to write the post, to come into this awareness. If so, we could be done here, right? No actual posting needed. I asked the Creator: *Can you give me another coin please so I know that I'm done here?*

I looked around the house. No coins anywhere. Instead, the ideas were still forthcoming. Things like creating links within the post page and PayPal buttons. Darn it. Wasn't this a bit too much for an active neurological impairment?

It is a good idea for me to stretch my brain a bit in order to exercise it. What's not a good stretch? The intense frustration I feel when I sit down intending to do something, then get confused, then try to force my way through it. There's a fine line between a good stretch and blowing the circuitry.

I decided I would try. But first, since I'm often unable to see errors or be confident that I've followed a train of thought, my writing should be professionally edited. A good friend who is a writer volunteered to edit my post and I felt myself relax. I had bought some time.

Wrong.

He reviewed it and sent it back immediately, calling it a remarkably clean edit. I was shocked.

Something was definitely going on.

I decided to take another step and set about the task of transferring my writing to WordPress and formatting it. Next, I slowly allowed myself to relearn some technical stuff so I could follow through with the suggestions given earlier.

Staying in the moment, I found each thing I "tried" came together steadily and remarkably without internal brain drama. *Somebody pinch me*, I thought. *This is a BIG DEAL!*

A hush came over me. I often stop to marvel at life's happenings, which is, I believe, what opens up the space for spiritual insight.

I finally accepted without a shadow of a doubt that I was meant to tell my story. But, since I'm the inquiring type, I couldn't help but wonder — *why*?

It was time to rest my brain. Taking a break, I sat down on the couch to rejuvenate myself with an episode of Super Soul Sunday. Oprah's guest was author Brené Brown. I didn't know Brené. Yet as she began to speak of courage and vulnerability, I felt she was talking to me like only a kindred spirit could.

The truth is, I don't know if this actually happened or if I'm delusional. I've since gone back and tried to find the part of the episode where Brené says these words and couldn't. On that particular day, as I watched I heard her say something along these lines: *She doesn't know why she writes about the stuff that she does, but she thinks part of her gift might be putting words to things that others feel and can relate to.*

I felt a sense of knowing come over me. I'm very aware that there's a sea of people with chronic illness. Maybe my post could help someone else by giving voice to a shared experience? Finally! I felt like I had my answer and felt so much better. The purpose had to be about more than me.

Before hitting the publish button that day, I intentionally let all thoughts about it go with a final prayer: *I release all attachment to the outcome. I won't wonder any more about the purpose of the post and I will wait for you, my loving Creator, to reveal to me what it is I need to know.*

Peace came, along with a sprinkle of joy. Little did I know how much love would follow."

That was the end of my post.

## *Were You Able to Spot the Chain of Affirmations?*

○ Three different coin events.

○ The ease of writing a very long blog post when I had not been able to write for months.

○ The ability to relearn my website so I could

post.

- o The ability to relearn and add more advanced things like links within the post and PayPal buttons.

- o A friend who volunteered on the spot to edit it.

- o The same friend sending it back immediately.

- o It was a very clean edit, with no additional work needed.

- o The answer to my last question of *why?* arrived almost immediately and gave me a sense of purpose; that the post, in all its vulnerability, might possibly help others. That put it in alignment with what I feel my calling is, making it easier for me to follow through.

- o All of this occurring in one day. I'd have been lucky if all of this could have come together in a few months' time with my best effort to focus.

Basically, the whole day was a complete anomaly in my life at the time. A chorus of affirmations including coins. A miracle.

## Spiritual Insight:
## Enhance Your Ability to Feel and Sense

Years ago, I took an intense, emotional course based in authenticity. My goal was to break through limiting beliefs and come into the awareness of any core issues that may prevent healing.

One of the exercises we did every time we reconvened to our circle after doing independent activities was a "check in." We were encouraged to put words to how we felt. This simple exercise had a lot to teach me.

Initially, what came to me were shallow answers. As time passed and my comfort level increased, "I'm ok" or "I'm fine" progressed to "I'm aware of some fearful thoughts, AND I feel calm in this room with you loving people, AND I'm anxious about going home tonight, AND I feel kind of giggly, AND I'm excited about the next thing we're doing, AND my head and back hurts."

How complex we are as humans. Who knew I could be fearful, calm, anxious, and giggly at the same time, in addition to excited and in physical pain, all at the same time? This class unlocked some very helpful insight and led to a deeper ability to work within my senses.

Your investment in the types of activities that

follow, over time, will unlock a whole other level of insight for you to work with. To start, sit quietly and run through your body parts while asking yourself questions such as:

- How does my head feel right now? How does my stomach feel, my shoulders, etc.? Is anything sore?

- Am I ignoring any symptoms in my body? Is there anything my physical body is telling me?

  **After sensing the physical body, run through the emotional senses. Ask yourself:**

- How do I feel emotionally right now? List everything.

  (Please allow yourself the freedom to contradict yourself. Yes, you can feel calm and at the same time be nervous about tomorrow's presentation at work. As divinely complex creatures, humans have the ability to hold multiple sensations that totally contradict each other. I've learned that discomfort arises from telling ourselves that we should not be that way.)

- Is there anything bothering me? Any conversation I need to have that would help me feel more harmonious within.

o What was the best moment of my day? What was the feeling in the moment that made it special?

o Breathe deeply. How does that deep breath feel?

## *Spiritual Insight: More Feeling/Sensing Exercises*

After watching a TV show, rather than moving onto the next thing, close your eyes and check in with your body. How is your internal world processing what you watched? How did you feel about it?

The TV is a great place to start, because the shows you watch do affect your senses. What if you learn that your favorite show, one that intrigues your mind, actually makes your body feel exhausted afterward? Wouldn't that be good information to realize?

You may learn that some shows feel like a waste of time, bring you down, or trigger you into the drama of past events. Conversely, other shows may remind you of how much you love your parents, treasure your best friends, need to get out into nature, or are longing to have a dog.

There's no judgment about what comes up. It's all simply data for consideration. Throw yourself into developing your senses and you'll find that your entire day is a treasure chest of information.

- o How do you feel after that phone call at work?

- o How do you feel when you finish a big project?

- o After you have lunch with a friend?

- o After you plan your vacation?

- o After you spend time with family?

The longer you pay attention, the easier it is to notice the subtleties and nuances. Information about how you feel is information about who you really are and what matters to you. It's the start of creating a life on purpose, rather than allowing life to just be "the same as it ever was."

When you tap into your feelings rather than running on autopilot, you begin to uncover some major, enlightening data about whether you're living authentically. Do your daily activities feed your soul? If not, where can you add in what does? These are the types of questions that more life satisfaction is birthed from.

Now it's time for our closing chapter. Turn the page for some parting thoughts on how to enjoy the process.

## Chapter 9

# ✧ Enjoy the Wonder

I realize that even with all the messages contained in this book, there will still be folks with specific circumstances who find themselves wondering what their messages in the coins are. One such circumstance would be the story that follows. It's an example of a unique situation that could warrant a little research to comprehend all it may have to offer.

## *Frank's Story: Curious Formations*

Thank you to Frank Spencer for sharing this intriguing occurrence.

"Last week I woke up and went into the hall to go to the kitchen. As I took a step, something caught my eye. On the floor in the middle of the hall were coins.

Three quarters, three dimes, and three pennies. All heads up.

The quarters were in a row vertically, the

dimes and pennies were set in a triangle around the top and bottom quarter.

I was crazy freaking out. Even more so when I realized that it was January 8th, so the date is a 1 and 8 and the amount of money totaled $1.08.

I felt much better when I came to your blog and started reading posts like these. It's a good thing, a message. I would like to know if there is a specific message due to the arrangement of the coins?"

**My answer to Frank went something like this:**

It's one of those stories almost too hard to believe, even for a believer. My favorite kind!

When you ask if there's something specific due to the arrangement, my guess is that having an order to the coins is "the invitation."

Maybe you've been very focused, or serious, or caught in the drudgery of daily life lately? I would interpret it as an invitation to return to a state of wonder—to be a kid again, believe in special experiences, magical messages, gifts from your Creator and loving messages from passed-on loved ones.

I also suggest researching the symbolism of the number 108, as well as the shape that was made with the coins, which you can easily do on Google. As you research, pay attention to any "knowing" that comes over you, any information that feels right, or just feels better.

I think you'll be interested to find that 108 is a positive number with sacred meaning attached to it in certain cultures.

From my intuitive perspective, the number 108 is associated with your beliefs and mindset around abundance. It affirms you are safe to trust your Creator to bring you abundance and suggests that you can be a positive influence on others to believe the same thing.

If you've temporarily been off track with your thoughts, it could be a gentle reminder to return your thoughts to believing in abundance once again.

If you're a person like Frank, with a mind-blowing coin story, and you feel in your gut that there's more to it than what's been offered here, my parting advice follows.

Consider everything about the circumstances: the time, the place they were found, the amount of the coin(s), the picture on it, the date on it, and the energy of it.

How did it make you feel? Were you amused? Were you awed? Did someone come to mind? Did a memory pop in? All things physical and emotional could be considered a clue.

If you've got a little detective streak in you, sorting out a message will probably be fun. If you're the perfectionist type, you stand the chance of getting more serious about it than it's supposed to be.

Remember, this is about wonder and fun. If awe gets traded for the obsession of "doing it right," uh...then, you're doing it wrong (she says with a smile).

Messages are based in love. They are meant to uplift. Be sure to keep it lighthearted.

It's also not complicated, so please keep it easy for yourself. Run through the messages in the book and if your divine filter rings true on something you read, you don't need to keep searching. That only muddies the water. Trust in that divine filter of yours and believe what you first feel is right!

If you begin to regularly pick up coins and things don't suddenly seem crystal clear; if you find yourself wondering, *Did I manage to begin a divine conversation?* Give it time. Just keep picking them up and paying attention to your impressions. Try putting them in a special jar. Patterns develop and more is often revealed over time.

The awesome thing about finding coins and considering whether there's a message is that participation is harmless. No harm is done if you feel like you received financial reassurance instead of thinking that a loved one said hello. Your loved one will give it another go.

It won't hurt any of us to do a life review by checking in with ourselves to see if we're in harmony with the path we're currently on. And it certainly won't hurt you to look for the wonder in things.

So please, I invite you...look for the wonder in ALL things and enjoy the process!

# ✧ Share the Love

I was talking with a trusted friend recently about getting ready to release this book into the world. When I called it "a book about love and wonder," tears came to his eyes and he said, "The world needs that so badly right now."

When my editor returned the manuscript after editing, she said it was "a joy to read through," and also went on to share a touching dime story that occurred during the period she had it for review. I cried. I felt hope well up in my heart. With every part of my being I hope that YOU, the reader, will feel uplifted—that a sense of joy will touch you.

I've often pondered why my brain would allow for writing at certain times and not others. Why now—for the last few months—was I finally able to assemble the manuscript? Perhaps there's a reason.

With so much going on in the world that feels fear-inducing and tragic, we offer sustenance to our spirits when we nurture our awareness of what's wondrous and love-filled in our world. It's a vital counterbalance. I'm thankful that the time has finally come that I may now make a contribution.

This is a self-published book, which means that my marketing team consists of you and me.

If I have earned your recommendation, I'd be honored if you'd help me spread the word so the book has a better chance of making it into the hands of those who may benefit from reading it. The easiest ways to help the book reach others are:

- o Talk to others about it. Tell your friends how you felt about it.

- o Give a copy to those people who you think could use a little wonder in their life.

- o Post a review online at sites like Amazon, Goodreads, Google Books, or Barnes and Noble. (When I'm considering whether to buy a book, a review from a previous buyer letting me know that the book impacted them in a positive way impacts my decision to buy!)

A big THANK YOU from me to you! I'm so grateful that you bought, read, and spent time with this book.

# ✧ Gratitude

Thank you to those who contacted me with their stories and allowed them to be included in this book. What a privilege and honor it is to share in the awe of your special moments.

I'm blessed to have these love anchors in my life:

Christopher, each day I think I already know the ways I'm blessed by your presence and each day even more is revealed. Thank you for constantly reflecting a higher form of love back to me.

My sisters—all the ladies of Eastside, especially Sue M., Teri S., Jeannie K., Amber S., and Jo P., as well as Tracy N.B., Denise L.G., Patty H., and Florence C., thank you for being a part of my life; for accepting me as I am, and for continuing to offer your friendship, love, and support. Knowing that you're still there, even if I seem to disappear, has made a world of difference to my emotional state. I'm smiling in your direction.

Thank you to all who've been on this healing journey with me—both in person and online. Your donations for healing treatments, heartfelt messages, and prayers have nourished my spirit during challenging times. What I've learned from you is that no matter how small life appears to be, there's still meaning to be found. Whether we are living large or small, we are all still students of life. We can still learn something right where we are, grow as a person, find purpose in helping others, experience love, and be the love we wish to see in the world.

Thank you to Jeanice R. There aren't enough words to express my gratitude for you and all that you've taught me. You're a role model of friendship and compassion that I'm humbled by. My heart smiles every time I think of you.

Not last by any means, thank you to my mother, Jean. Your love has been the one constant in my life. Your belief that I'm here to make a difference in this world has never wavered. It's helped me believe that I'm not done here yet. I'm so thankful for the ways our relationship continues to evolve. You are precious and you are loved.

# ✧ About the Author

Kimberly Ahri was a successful business woman when, at the age of thirty-seven, she experienced a dramatic "course correction" in her life. Conditions changed at tornado speed and she was stripped bare of the facade she had built to give herself an identity.

With only shreds of a "normal" life left, Kimberly found herself on a journey with angels. This odyssey, replete with experience, loss, and love, took her through an emotional masterclass on what truly matters in life. The spiritual curriculum required that she look deep within and allow the emergence of her intuitive gifts so she could honor her purpose in this world.

Although she's an intensely private person, she writes and shares openly about the divine tutelage she's blessed to perceive and advocates for love, compassion, honor, and wonder.

She's a health researcher and hope addict; a lover of clean food, clean breathing, sunshine, the ocean, the scenery and good people of Newfoundland, almond milk lattes, sourdough bread and real butter.

Kimberly can be reached online, where you may also find information about her other works:

Facebook: Author Kimberly Ahri
Twitter: @KimberlyAhri

Made in the USA
Middletown, DE
08 April 2018